T0355890

WADE DAVIS

BENEATH
THE SURFACE OF THINGS

NEW AND SELECTED ESSAYS

GREYSTONE BOOKS
Vancouver/Berkeley/London

Greystone Books Ltd.
greystonebooks.com

Cataloguing data available from Library and Archives Canada
ISBN 978-1-77840-283-8 (pbk.)
ISBN 978-1-77840-044-5 (cloth)
ISBN 978-1-77840-043-8 (epub)

Editing by Nancy Flight
Copy editing by Crissy Calhoun
Proofreading by Jennifer Stewart
Cover and text design by Jessica Sullivan
Cover photograph by cokada/iStock

Printed and bound in Canada on FSC® certified paper at Friesens. The FSC® label means that materials used for the product have been responsibly sourced.

Greystone Books thanks the Canada Council for the Arts, the British Columbia Arts Council, the Province of British Columbia through the Book Publishing Tax Credit, and the Government of Canada for supporting our publishing activities.

MIX
Paper | Supporting
responsible forestry
FSC® C016245

Canada

BRITISH COLUMBIA | BRITISH COLUMBIA ARTS COUNCIL
An agency of the Province of British Columbia

Canada Council   Conseil des arts
for the Arts   du Canada

Greystone Books gratefully acknowledges the xʷməθkʷəy̓əm (Musqueam), Sḵwx̱wú7mesh (Squamish), and səlilwətaɬ (Tsleil-Waututh) peoples on whose land our Vancouver head office is located.

For Cade, the new light
in a grandfather's eye

CONTENTS

INTRODUCTION

I ONCE ASKED THE POET Gary Snyder to name the single most important thing we could do to support the wild. He replied, "Stay put." Sure enough, in the early months of 2020, as travel came to an end and the world shut down, nature rebounded in a manner that was both astonishing and profoundly hopeful. Overnight, or so it seemed, caïmans once again darkened the sands of Baja, wild boars moved through the streets of Barcelona, flamingos by the thousands gathered in the wetlands of Mumbai, wolves and bears returned to the valley floor at Yosemite. Rivers ran through Medellín and Bogotá as if mountain streams. The canals of Venice were clear for the first time in modern memory. Slum dwellers long shrouded in smoke and industrial haze in Delhi, Lahore, and Kathmandu woke to blue skies and white mountain summits scoring the horizons. In a time of global fear and peril, the resilience of nature unveiled the promise of a new dream of the Earth.

In the end, of course, nature was not reborn, and as the pandemic waned, old habits returned with a haste and confidence that was itself haunting. That so many had suffered, with millions having perished, was lost in the fluidity of our memory, overwhelmed by our capacity as a species to forget. What we recall as individuals is not the planetary but the deeply personal, all the crazy anecdotes that we've shared with each other over these last many months. Where we were and what we were doing as the world skidded to a halt and all our precious plans took a sharp detour to the car wash.

Returning from Colombia in the first days of March 2020, I was looking ahead to a travel schedule that would have me in seven countries, speaking at some forty events through the end of May. A new book was to be launched in April, with media appearances already booked for Canada, the U.S., and the U.K. On the day that Italy shut down and Israel closed the international airport in Tel Aviv, my wife, Gail, and I very nearly boarded a flight for Amman, with a dozen elderly Canadians in our charge, all over seventy-five and all keen to tour the ancient sites of Jordan. Instead, with immense relief, we hunkered down on our little island near Vancouver, like schoolchildren who had stumbled upon a summer vacation they hadn't expected. A vacation that morphed into a retreat that ran on for two years.

Time became something new. Life slowed down. Work became leisure, with new and unexpected efficiencies that, in the short term, were truly liberating. I recall one morning in particular, early in the lockdown. From my office on the hill, I began the day online with an editor at *Rolling Stone* in New York, honing one of the essays featured in this collection, "The Unraveling of America." I then reached out to a colleague in Toronto to finalize edits of a short essay on Lawren Harris, scheduled for an upcoming book on the Group of Seven. Using Zoom for the first time, I delivered a talk at a writers festival in California, addressing not three hundred attendees but an online audience of four thousand, all without having to spend three days drinking in excess while chatting up strangers. I then moved on to Singapore, administering remotely a makeup exam for one of my students. His results in hand, graded and submitted to the university, I glanced at my watch. It was not yet noon. Just enough time to plant the apple saplings before lunch, which I happily did, in a meadow flush with wildflowers.

For well on a year, forced like everyone to stay put, I embraced stillness and before long was looking back at my old frenetic life of travel as if a violent hallucination. Almost everything I'd previously written had been based on movement, direct experiences at the far ends of the Earth. Suddenly travel was not an option. I had no choice but to take in the world through the windows of this small aerie on the hill, explorations that carried me not along rivers or across deserts but through dense forests of words in texts that opened new vistas, encouraging me to think and write in new ways. Books took the place of ethnographic expeditions. Writing was a way of making sense of the whirlwind of solitude that had become our lives.

The essays in this new collection, written for the most part during the months of the pandemic lockdown, cover a great deal of ground, from war and race to mountains, plants, climate, exploration, the promise of youth, and the essence of the sacred. They are linked less by theme than by circumstance. They all came about during the unhurried months when one who had traveled incessantly was obliged to stay still, even as events flared on all sides in a world that never stops moving.

One of the more notable contributions in the collection, "The Unraveling of America," exemplifies the serendipitous, even accidental, manner by which so many of these essays came about. Early in the pandemic, invited by several editors and publications to write about the crisis, I hesitated, uncertain that I had anything new to contribute. Then one summer evening late in July, as I paddled a kayak around our island, it struck me that the pandemic was less a story of medicine and public health than one of history and culture.

Over the next two days, I wrote seven thousand words, which went off unsolicited to an old friend, Jann Wenner, founder of *Rolling Stone*. Jann shared the piece with his son Gus, who passed it on to his editorial team. After some clever reworking, it was posted on the *Rolling Stone* website on August 6, 2020. Within six weeks, it had attracted five million readers and generated 362 million social media impressions. Media interest in the story was sustained over many weeks, with interview requests coming in from twenty-three countries and from outlets across the political spectrum. In a bizarre juxtaposition, I spoke with Hari Sreenivasan of PBS on one day and on the next did an interview with Steve Bannon in his *War Room* the morning before his notorious arrest.

Written in the heat of the moment, the essay got some things right and some things wrong. With the re-election of Donald Trump a distinct possibility, the plight of America at the time looked especially grim. Canada, by contrast, appeared that summer to be escaping the worst of the pandemic, which it most assuredly did not, though its performance was consistently better than that of its neighbor. No vaccine had been developed in less than four years; few imagined that science would deliver a new class of effective vaccines in a matter of months, as if to affirm the very notion of American exceptionalism that the essay calls into question.

Although some may have read the piece as an indictment, I wrote it as an intervention. If a family member is in trouble, the first act is to hold up a mirror to let them see how far they have fallen, which is the beginning of the path to rehabilitation and recovery. The essay attracted a global readership, I'd like to think, not because it served up an anti-American diatribe but because, quite to the contrary, it was free of polemics, unburdened by ideology, and written with real concern and empathy for a nation that had made my own life possible. Loved ones often disappoint, and if America hasn't broken your heart, as Cory Booker writes, then you don't love her enough.

Several of the other essays in the collection are published here for the first time: "The Promised Land," "Beyond Climate Fear and Trepidation," "A Message to a Daughter," and "Mother India." Others have previously appeared in various publications. "The Art of Exploring" first ran in the *Financial Times* (September 2, 2020); "Why Anthropology Matters" in *Scientific American* (February 1, 2021); "This Is America" in the *Literary Review of Canada* (July–August 2021); "The Divine Leaf of Immortality" on Alexander (2021); "A New Word for Indigenous" in the *Globe and Mail* (March 25, 2023). "The Crowning of Everest" appeared in 2021 as the introduction to the Folio Society's two-volume *Everest: From Reconnaissance to Summit, 1921 to 1953*. "On the Sacred" was originally written for *Sacred*, a large-format illustrated book published by Insight Editions in 2022. "War and Remembrance" appeared in the commemorative anthology *In Flanders Fields: 100 Years; Writing on War, Loss and Remembrance*, published by Knopf Canada in 2015.

I most assuredly did not write these essays with a book in mind. Eclectic would be too generous a term for such a seemingly random selection of topics and themes. But as I worked through the idea with Nancy Flight, my editor and good friend at Greystone, she discerned a consistent point of view that brought to mind something that one of my great mentors, the late Johannes Wilbert, once told me.

A professor of anthropology at UCLA, Johannes had lived and worked among the Winikina Warao in the Orinoco delta of Venezuela for more than forty years. As a graduate student, I would fly from Boston to Los Angeles just for the chance to spend a weekend with him at his cabin in the San Gabriel Mountains, as his mind ranged across the entire field of anthropology, sessions that invariably left me mentally exhausted but intellectually on fire. He was a gifted teacher, with a way of distilling the grandest notions in a phrase.

"Anthropology," he would say, "reveals what lies beneath the surface of things." It calls not for the elimination of judgment, only its suspension, so that the judgments we are all ethically obliged to make as human beings may be informed ones. At its best, the anthropological lens allows us to see, and perhaps seek, the wisdom in the middle way, a perspective of promise and hope that all of the essays in this collection aspire to convey.

1

THIS IS AMERICA

ONE OF THE JOYS of living in Washington, D.C., was the promise of spring days with the cherry blossoms in bloom and friends arriving from out of town, all of them keen to experience the great monuments and sweeping vistas of the nation's capital. Even the most jaded among them—modern architects, for example, who dismissed the entire city as a neo-classical theme park—could not mask their emotions when standing in the historic shadow of Martin Luther King Jr., pausing on the stone steps that overlook the still waters of the Reflecting Pool, or staring at a black granite wall, polished to a mirror finish, as aging vets and heartbroken mothers reached out to touch the names of brothers and loved ones lost in the jungles of Vietnam. I took both pride and care in gently curating our outings, knowing from experience how much visitors could take, both physically and emotionally.

We began always with Maya Lin's dark masterpiece and then, passing over Korea, much as history has done, made our way to the Lincoln Memorial. On one wall, etched in limestone, is the Gettysburg Address—the English language compressed to perfection. Equally inspired is the president's First Inaugural Address, written for a nation torn by secession but not yet at war. Invoking "the mystic chords of memory," Abraham Lincoln beseeched all Americans, north and south, to take time and reach for the "better angels of our nature." That the country ignored his plea is etched in sorrow upon his face, carved in marble, in a massive sculpture that sits steady in repose, gazing half the length of the National Mall to the Washington Monument, which dominates the ceremonial heart of the capital. The axis mundi of democracy, it is the tallest stone structure in the world, dwarfing any obelisk ever conceived by the pharaohs of Egypt.

The monument stands on the heights of a broad, grassy knoll, surrounded at the base by a circle of flags that represent the fifty states of the union, its pyramidal capstone seeming to soar into the heavens. No building in Washington is allowed to be taller. Though built to honor the first president, it visually recalls the trials of the sixteenth, martyred and murdered in the wake of a national crisis that brought construction to a halt for twenty years. A distinct break in coloration—lighter below, darker above—marks where work stopped and was later resumed, as if the entire nation in the interlude had been indelibly stained by the blood of fratricidal war.

Across the Potomac River, some distance away, a hill rises to the mansion portico where Robert E. Lee once paced, lost in thought as he struggled to decide whether to command the Union army, at Lincoln's request, or to serve the Confederate cause. History recalls his torment: loyal to the nation, yet incapable of betraying his beloved state of Virginia. Lee's rebel forces would fight the Union for five years, in battles that left tens of thousands of dead. Many would be buried on land confiscated from Lee and his family, the only sanction to

befall a man whose choice of sedition was singularly responsible for prolonging a war that brought misery to millions.

After Lincoln and all his sorrows, we would stroll around
the Tidal Basin to reach the steps of the Jefferson Memorial, perhaps the most moving of all the monuments, both in
design and in the power of its message. Just to stand in the
cool shade of its soaring vault, with Thomas Jefferson's words
inscribed on white marble, is to rekindle a childlike faith in
the great experiment that began a century before the agonies
of civil war.

Etched in the frieze below the dome is the perfect distil-
lation of the Enlightenment: "I have sworn upon the altar of
God eternal hostility against every form of tyranny over the
mind of man." The words are taken from a letter that Jefferson sent to the doctor Benjamin Rush, in 1800, in which he
rejects both state religion and the very notion of absolute
faith, accepting belief in God but heralding rational inquiry,
the triumph of reason over myth, science over magic.

Intellectual emancipation, the defining spirit of the age,
resonates in another passage that has long served as the
moral charter of the United States, the second line of the
Declaration of Independence: "We hold these truths to be self-
evident, that all men are created equal, that they are endowed
by their Creator with certain unalienable rights, among these
are life, liberty, and the pursuit of happiness, that to secure
these rights, governments are instituted among men."

Finally, there is this: "I tremble for my country when I
reflect that God is just, that His justice cannot sleep forever.
Commerce between master and slave is despotism. Nothing
is more certainly written in the book of fate than that these
people are to be free."

These three statements, penned by the same hand, all breathlessly inspiring, nevertheless stumble over each other in a bundle of contradictions. In anticipating a great reckoning, as if willing into being the wrath of a God whose power he has rejected, Jefferson acknowledges slavery in a manner that, on the face of it, appears to challenge the very premise of the Declaration of Independence, as if suggesting such a foundational document had been disingenuous from its inception. How can a nation born in liberty tolerate human bondage? The dedication to inquiry so famously celebrated by the minds of the Enlightenment guaranteed that such a contradiction could never be concealed; the truth would fester like an open sore.

Oddly enough, generations of Americans have found comfort in this confusion, grateful to know that Jefferson was at least aware of the conundrum and willing to acknowledge it in writing. Surely, such reasoning runs, the original sin of slavery was just one part of a whole, further evidence of the complex origins of a land of multitudes, then as now the best and worst of all things, a nation at odds with its past, yet always forging ahead toward a better tomorrow. Like so many, I long subscribed to this view, refusing to judge the past by the standards of today, at ease in the promise and contradictions that lie at the heart of the American experience.

Events over these last months have surely challenged such complacency, raising any number of disturbing questions, many of which are explored in a brilliant and widely heralded book by the Harvard historian Jill Lepore. In *These Truths: A History of the United States*, she calls for a wrenching re-examination of the very idea of America. As surely as Dorothy's dog, Toto, reveals the true identity of the Wizard of

Oz, Lepore with both empathy and insight pulls back the veil on American history, leaving us with no choice but to think anew. What if the very language of freedom, for example, that gave birth to the United States of America had always been intended for whites alone? What if the nation was established on the presumption of racial supremacy, as if it were a law of nature, such that the universal rights of man as perceived by the founding fathers had, from their perspective, nothing whatsoever to do with the everyday atrocity of slavery? What if the disconnect we now recognize was not even an issue for Jefferson and his peers? If so, what does this say about America, and how might it explain events that haunt us to this day?

In trembling for his country, Thomas Jefferson did not advocate emancipation. His anticipation of the judgment of history, so solemnly spoken, did not stop him from mortgaging 140 of his own slaves with a Dutch bank to secure funds to build his palatial home at Monticello, in Virginia. When George Washington presided over the 1787 convention that established the U.S. Constitution, he remained a handsome, even heroic, figure, save for his terrible teeth, which had been replaced with dentures made of wood and human ivory, nine teeth torn from the mouths of his living slaves. James Madison, who drafted the Constitution, complained that in order to buy a collection of books essential to his research, he had been obliged to sell a slave who had been his property since Madison himself had been but a child. And even as Abraham Lincoln, in 1861, invoked angels and called for compassion and kindness, he assured his fellow Americans that he was not inclined to interfere with slavery in the Southern states and had every intention of enforcing the Fugitive Slave Act of 1850, which mandated that any escaped slave, captured in any state of the union, would be forcibly returned to bondage. Angels, mystic chords, and iron shackles.

Many years ago, on a journey through West Africa, an American journalist and highly regarded colleague from the National Geographic Society casually remarked, as if stating a law of nature, that race is the story of America. At the time I didn't believe it could be so simple, but lately I've wondered.

THE ENGLISH CAME LATE to the Americas. The Spaniards founded St. Augustine in 1565, Santa Fe in 1607. The French reached the island of Montreal in 1534 and by 1608 were building a fortress to dominate the St. Lawrence River at Quebec. Sir Walter Raleigh sent an expedition to the outer banks of North Carolina only in 1585. The following spring, Sir Francis Drake, with three hundred Africans in chains, arrived to resupply the fledging settlement, only to find everyone desperate to leave. To make room on his ship, he was obliged to dump his unwanted cargo into the sea. Also left behind in the sand were the pathogens that would conquer a continent. When John Winthrop, founder of the Massachusetts Bay Colony, arrived but a generation later, he noted with pleasure that smallpox had swept away the Native people, a sure sign of divine intervention that allowed him to occupy an empty land as righteously as Abraham had displaced the Sodomites.

Winthrop and his Puritans were spiritual outliers, cut from the same cloth as many who washed ashore in those early years, members of sects that England denied and persecuted, zealots who came to America in search of freedom so that they might practice, without interference, their own forms of religious intolerance. Theirs was a dream of Zion. The inconvenient presence of people native to the land was resolved by disease, which ultimately killed 90 percent of the Indigenous population. Those who survived were erased from history, as colonists invoked Aristotle to argue that those who did not own the land in any manner recognizable to an Englishman were by nature slaves. Terra nullius—land belonging to nobody—was a fiction, but in time it both rationalized and propelled the settlement of a continent, and with it the dispossession and death of millions.

The colonial experience in New France was very different. There, in a northern land with more lakes than people, where winter dictated the mood, mercantile zeal drove an economy based on a fashion statement, the beaver hat. For its first 240 years, what would become Canada was not a settler society; it became such only in the mid-nineteenth century. The early French and later the Scots were by no means kind to Indigenous communities, but they never set out to slaughter them. Alliances with First Nations were essential to a trade that was, from the start, dependent on their knowledge and skills. As John Ralston Saul has written, the fur traders did not murder the Indians; they married them and in doing so moved up in the world.

To the south, the Spaniards had even less interest in settlement. Their imperial regime was based on extraction, plunder made possible by the wealth of the vanquished, the stolen treasures of a continent. The Crown deliberately mired its colonies in ignorance, if only to better exert control. Books and newspapers of any but Spanish origins were banned. No colonial subject could possess a printing press. By law, no man born in the colonies could own a mine or a vineyard, grow tobacco or olive trees, plant grapes or sell goods in the street, or trade in gold, silver, copper, pearls, or emeralds, in leather, sugar, cotton, or wool, even in basic foods such as potatoes and tomatoes. None could travel without permission.

Such oppression implied torment for the poor, degradation and dishonor for the rich, all but guaranteeing that in time the people would come together as a single revolutionary force, as they did in 1812 under Simón Bolívar, who forged an army from runaway slaves, landed gentry, and landless peasants. Miscegenation was the norm. As early as 1775, free Blacks outnumbered the enslaved throughout the Spanish possessions. Tradition dictated that the wealthy, with an eye to God, liberate their slaves in their wills. Complete emancipation came in 1826, a decade after Bolívar had freed his own slaves, something Washington did only at his death; Jefferson and Madison never did it at all.

Their America was all about settlement and always had been—settlement and slavery. Natives captured in war were sold in bondage to Caribbean plantations, including the nine-year-old son of Metacom, the great Wampanoag sachem who was drawn and quartered in Plymouth in 1676, his head mounted on a pike. Africans in shackles, crammed into holds slippery with blood and vomit, and great stores of indigo, tobacco, hides, and sugar to yield molasses and rum: these were the products of the Atlantic trade, a triangle of exchange that propelled the growth of all the colonies. There was no north and south. Half the wealth of New England was derived from sugar grown on West Indian plantations worked by the enslaved.

In Virginia, liberty and slavery came into the world as if siblings, born in the same year, 1619, as landowners met in a legislative body, the House of Burgesses, and the first Africans came ashore in chains at Point Comfort. The Puritans of Massachusetts, the Dutch of New York, the Quakers of Pennsylvania all exploited slave labor. In the early years of the eighteenth century, half the households of New York possessed slaves; by 1776, they were fully a quarter of the population. The original wall for which Wall Street is named was built by the enslaved to enclose the site of slave auctions. The city itself is named for the Duke of York, the future king and founder of the Company of Royal Adventurers, an innocent name for an enterprise that carried three thousand Africans a year to Barbados and Jamaica, each branded on the breast with the initials D.Y. In 1738 in Philadelphia, Benjamin Franklin published one of the first books to rage against the evils of the trade; at the time, he was himself the owner of three slaves, Joseph, a boy, and Peter and Jemima, husband and wife.

The Revolutionary War presented a rhetorical challenge. In declaring that "all men are by nature free and independent," George Mason, who drafted the Virginia Declaration of Rights, added the caveat that such inherent rights accrue only to those who "enter into a state of society." Naturally, since Africans would never have a place in society, they had no claim to liberty. Such intellectual contortions were convenient but complicated, especially as the British guaranteed freedom to any enslaved man who joined the king's armies to help suppress the rebellion.

Madison's grandfather had been poisoned by a slave. Washington's slaves had been running away for a generation. During the war, the number of fugitives soared, as roughly one in five Africans, 100,000 altogether, tried desperately to reach the British forces; pregnant women, in particular, yearned to give birth behind the lines so that their children might be granted certificates of freedom. The colonial oppressor was, in fact, the facilitator of freedom. Washington responded by calling for a careful accounting of loss so that owners might seek compensation for "property" carried off in British ships. He stood by as some five thousand enslavers scoured New York. Many freedom seekers were caught, including a fifteen-year-old girl who was given eighty lashes, her punishment made worse by hot embers poured into her wounds. Others perished, including fifteen of the thirty who had fled Jefferson's plantation. Altogether some twenty thousand made it, including 5,327 who sailed out of Charleston, South Carolina, even as the city celebrated the British defeat.

WITH AMERICAN FREEDOM and independence, the enslaved population surged, the dark commerce prospering as never before: more than a million Africans arrived in the first decade of the young nation's life, the largest importation in the history of the trade. While some states acknowledged the long shadow of the heinous institution, with talk of abolition growing even in the South, business and the banks doubled down on the profits to be made, especially as cotton boomed.

In 1791, the second of the great American revolutions broke out in the French colony of Saint-Domingue. War raged until 1804, when Haitian patriots, having defeated the finest armies of Napoleon, finally declared their independence. The United States had done everything possible to aid the French; arms, ammunition, and money flowed to the desperate colonial planters. Jefferson dismissed Haitians as "cannibals," warning Madison that should such fury reach their shores, there would be much to fear. What Bolívar saw as a war of liberation—the Haitian government in time would fund his revolution on the condition that he free the slaves of Gran Colombia—Jefferson viewed as the first successful slave revolt in history. It was, of course, both. Many plantation owners fleeing the wreckage of Saint-Domingue found their way to the land opening up in Mississippi and Louisiana, where they rebuilt their lives in a flourishing slave economy. They brought with them tales of horror, bloodshed, rape, and pillage that steeled many a Southern heart, setting back the cause of emancipation for generations.

A moment that ought to have marked the death of an era, the formal end of the Atlantic slave trade in 1808, was hardly noticed in a land where cotton was king and a booming domestic trade saw more than a million slaves from Virginia and the Carolinas shipped to the Deep South. By 1860, another million would be sent west. If slavery was the engine of the economy, cotton turned America into a financial juggernaut. Cotton was to the nineteenth century what oil became in the twentieth: the country's greatest export and the world's most valuable and widely traded commodity. Production doubled between 1815 and 1820 and doubled again by 1825. The value of slaves rose and fell with the price of bales quoted on the docks of Liverpool. Their bodies worked the fields but also created the plantations, felling vast swaths of forest, an endless process given the speed with which the crop laid waste to soils, with yields falling by the year, generating an endless demand for new land.

For this, the country had the right man in the right place at the right time. Andrew Jackson, hero of the Battle of New Orleans, was no military genius, but he knew how to kill Indians. And that was his goal—to rid the entire American Southeast of their presence. His campaigns against the

Seminoles, Chickasaw, Choctaw, and Creek were little more than massacres. One of his first acts as president was to push through the Indian Removal Act of 1830, which condemned sixty thousand men, women, and children to the Trail of Tears, a virtual death march that had the survivors trudging west to settlement camps beyond the Mississippi. The tribes were forced to abandon millions of acres of traditional lands that were taken over by the government, only to be sold on the cheap to speculators, settlers, and enslavers.

As forests fell, plantations spread and cotton yields skyrocketed. In 1831, the country harvested 350 million pounds, half the global production; four years later, the figure was 500 million pounds. The value of a young man sold on the auction block in New Orleans tripled in fifty years to some $1,600, roughly $50,000 today. Every year, as the plantations became more efficient and more systematized, demands on labor increased. A field hand picked four times as much cotton in a day in 1862 as his predecessor had done in 1800. Punishments reflected price fluctuations on the global markets. The key was the whip. A slave who ended the day five pounds short of his quota felt the deficit on his back—five lashes to make up for the lost production. It was an economy made possible by torture.

Looming over an expanding nation was always the problem of the West and the fate of new territories, all eager to achieve statehood. In 1848, in the wake of war, the country acquired a million square miles of what had been Mexico. America's destiny hinged on a recurring question: slave state or free? In Washington, politicians sought any number of compromises that only prolonged the agony. In a sop to the South, the Fugitive Slave Act of 1850 rendered no corner of the country safe for any person of color; bounty hunters made a business of seizing even those born free, to be sold into bondage. The Dred Scott decision of 1857, written by the country's chief justice, Roger Taney, determined that Congress could not limit the expansion of slavery into any state, on the grounds that the founding fathers who wrote the Constitution obviously considered Africans "beings of an inferior order, and altogether unfit to associate with the white race, either in social or political relations; and so far inferior, that they had no rights which the white man was bound to respect."

No "negro of the African race," Taney wrote, as if acknowledging the preposterous, could ever expect to claim the rights and privileges of citizenship. If vile, the decision was at least honest. The highest court in the land had denied even the possibility of equality. This was the beginning of the great reckoning. "You may close your Supreme Court against the black man's cry for justice, but you cannot, thank God, close against him the ear of a sympathising world, nor shut up the Court of Heaven," Frederick Douglass said of the decision. "Slavery lives in this country not because of any paper Constitution, but in the moral blindness of the American people."

Fear as much as greed now dominated the country. In 1859, the year John Brown rose up in open insurrection at Harpers Ferry, the state of Arkansas passed laws forcing all free Blacks to leave or suffer enslavement. Oregon, a free state, nevertheless instituted policies that segregated white from Black. In Washington, Congress invoked a rule banning debate on slavery, as if the topic was too explosive to discuss.

As the country moved toward civil war, Southern politicians left no doubt as to the essence of their cause. Even as Lincoln sought compromise, Jefferson Davis declared, "The condition of slavery is with us nothing but a form of civil government for a class of people not fit to govern themselves."

Anyone wishing to invoke states' rights (or who recalls the avuncular Shelby Foote reminding the filmmaker Ken Burns that most Southerners didn't own slaves and fought simply because the Yankees "was down here") ought to consider a speech delivered in Savannah by Alexander Stephens, the Confederate vice president, in which he clearly outlined the South's aims. Whereas the U.S. Constitution rested on an assumption of equality among the races, Stephens began, "our new Government is founded upon exactly the opposite ideas; its foundations are laid, its cornerstone rests, upon the great truth that the negro is not equal to the white man; that slavery... is his natural and moral condition. This, our new Government, is the first, in the history of the world, based on this great physical, philosophical and moral truth." The Confederacy was not motivated by the rights of states; it was founded on the idea of racial supremacy.

The soldiers on both sides knew the truth. "The fact that slavery is the sole undeniable cause of this infamous rebellion, that it is a war of, by, and for Slavery, is as plain as the noon-day sun," a Union soldier wrote in 1862. That same year, a Confederate wrote, "Any man who pretends to believe that this is not a war for the emancipation of the blacks ... is either a fool or a liar." Lincoln viewed slavery as an abomination, and he and some 360,000 Union soldiers offered up their lives to destroy the institution—a sacrifice that must surely inform any conversation about race in America, then or now.

But as a politician, he walked a fine line. "If I could save the Union without freeing any slave I would do it," he wrote in a letter to the newspaper editor Horace Greeley, "and if I could save it by freeing all the slaves I would do it... What I do about slavery, and the colored race, I do because I believe it helps to save the Union."

With his eye on military victory, Lincoln issued the Emancipation Proclamation in 1862, deliberately exempting the border states, which got to keep their slaves, thanks to their fidelity to the Union. Then, as now, there was nothing pure in politics. That same year, he invited a number of prominent Black leaders to the White House to discuss a scheme that would have all former slaves deported to Central America or shipped back to Africa, so certain was he that they'd never find a home in the United States.

The president's emotions, convictions, and calculations were as complex as the times in which he lived. But the Emancipation Proclamation, though excluding Maryland, Delaware, Kentucky, and Missouri, was a siren call of liberty, an irrevocable commitment that infused a struggling Northern cause with moral righteousness, while igniting a conflagration of hatred and fear throughout the South, which recognized such liberty as an existential threat. Mere possession of the document in the Confederacy was punishable by death.

But sanctions did nothing to stop the long march to freedom. Southern politicians and pastors, overseers and auctioneers, ordinary soldiers and exalted generals all shuddered as former slaves flocked to the Union colors and became an army within an army—186,000 men, each with memories of wickedness to avenge.

UNION VICTORY made possible the promise of a new nation. In the first years of Reconstruction, laws expanded civil liberties, prohibited racial discrimination, acknowledged a woman's right to property, mandated free education for all, and reduced the severity of criminal sanctions. The Fourteenth Amendment gave the vote to formerly enslaved men and granted citizenship to anyone born on American soil. Black voter turnout in local and state elections throughout the South reached an astonishing 90 percent. Hundreds served in local, state, and federal government. In Mississippi, where for generations the killing of a slave had not legally constituted murder, two Black men were elected to the U.S. Senate. In a flash of spirit and hope, an Alabama convention declared, "The law no longer knows white nor black, but simply men." Perhaps for a time, but not for long.

Mississippi proved to be a bellwether. A state that in 1866 dedicated fully a fifth of its budget to providing prosthetic limbs to veterans was not about to abandon its faith in the Southern cause nor in white supremacy. In neighboring Tennessee, the very ghosts of the Confederate dead rose as if from the grave, avengers clad in white robes, a cult of terror and insurrection that included the scions of society, men of wealth, education, and influence, riding together under the banner of the Ku Klux Klan. In Colfax, Louisiana, armed vigilantes set fire to the county courthouse, burning alive those within and murdering those who fled, leaving behind more than 150 broken and charred bodies as a message to anyone foolish enough to believe in legal rights and the sanctity of the Constitution.

Laws were upheld at the discretion of the powerful, and in the South, this implied a series of racial codes that effectively re-established the economics of slavery, only in the guise of indentured labor and sharecropping. Black workers who left their jobs forfeited wages and were subject to arrest. In South Carolina, any Black person who sought work not as a farmer or servant had to pay a tax equivalent to $1,600. Debt peonage bound sharecroppers to the very families and plantations that had worked them as slaves. Men convicted of meaningless charges—invented crimes such as vagrancy or mischief—were held in chains and leased at no pay to enterprises eager to exploit prison labor. Children entered white households to be educated, only to be worked morning to dusk as unpaid servants.

Southern legislatures everywhere targeted Black suffrage with literacy standards and poll taxes that disenfranchised voters so effectively that by 1950, a century after the passage of the Fugitive Slave Act, only 7 percent of Black people eligible to vote in Mississippi were registered to do so. Their voice in government was silenced. After John R. Lynch was defeated in 1882, nearly a century would pass before Mississippi sent another African American representative to Washington. Blanche Bruce, born enslaved in Virginia and elected as a senator from Mississippi in 1874, stepped down in 1881; eighty-six years would pass before an African American again served in the U.S. Senate. After P.B.S. Pinchback of Louisiana left office in 1873, the United States would not elect another Black governor until 1990.

In a nation famous for backroom deals, perhaps the most infamous occurred in 1876, when Rutherford Hayes, in exchange for support in his bid for the presidency, agreed to withdraw federal troops from the South. Though now long forgotten, this ardent abolitionist and valiant soldier, wounded five times while fighting for the Union, chose personal glory over duty at a fulcrum of history. Ending the military occupation implied the end of Reconstruction. Hayes's singular achievement as president was to reduce Blacks once again to servitude.

As the South rose from the ashes of defeat and humiliation, the horrors of slavery were subsumed by a new narrative—the Lost Cause. The war was reimagined as a story of sacrifice and honor, of men and boys dying to defend a way of life, an agrarian civilization far removed from immigrant hordes and industrial grime, where Blacks and whites knew their place in a land of contentment, order, and faith—all of it, as a novel and later a film would famously portray, gone with the wind. Central to the mythology was the notion that the Civil War had never really been about slavery; rather it was a battle for the rights of Southerners to defend their states, just as the Founding Fathers had envisioned in creating a federalist union. Viewed through this lens, the Confederacy had been the true heir of the American Revolution, its gallant armies, outnumbered in every battle, the forces of freedom, led by generals inspired by the gods—Stonewall Jackson, Jeb Stuart, James Longstreet, and Robert E. Lee.

The focus of adoration fell on Lee, deified in defeat as, in the words of one Southern journalist, "among the finest human beings that has ever walked the Earth." Remembered for his stoic dignity at Appomattox, his uncanny ability to vanquish vastly superior armies in the field, including a stunning series of victories at Manassas, Fredericksburg, and Chancellorsville that came close to winning the war, Lee was written into Southern history as a humble and decent Christian who personally abhorred slavery and who worked tirelessly in the wake of defeat to bring together a broken nation. In time, his name would grace churches and hotels, military forts and theaters, more than fifty schools and universities, some eighty streets and public highways, eight counties, and scores of town squares in both the South and the North. His untimely death, in 1870, prompted an outpouring of grief, together with a flurry of construction, as statues of Lee and all the other legends of the Confederate firmament went up across the South.

Further burnishing Lee's reputation was his familial connection to George Washington. His wife, Mary, was the daughter of George Washington Parke Custis, the adopted son of the first president. But here the myth runs up against the historical record. Through marriage, Lee took on responsibility for the Custis plantation. His first move was to break a long-standing family tradition of never separating enslaved families, hardly a gesture of grace for one said to be appalled by the institution. Within three years, in fact, Lee had broken up every family but one. Those who escaped only to be recaptured could expect the most brutal treatment, the lashings often administered by Lee himself, who insisted that brine be applied to the wounds.

At the outbreak of the Civil War, Lee was a serving officer in the U.S. Army. His loyalty was to his state, as the story goes, but his decision to fight for the South suggests that in his most fateful hour, white supremacy, the bedrock principle of the Confederacy, trumped fidelity to country. Throughout the war, notably during the two invasions that climaxed at Antietam in 1862 and Gettysburg the following summer, Lee insisted that any Black person captured in the North, whatever their status, be carried south and returned to bondage.

Black soldiers serving for the Union expected no quarter in battle; capture implied torture and death. Entire units were massacred.

Not once did Lee intervene. When Ulysses S. Grant, in the waning days of the war, proposed prisoner exchanges without reference to race, Lee refused, noting that "negroes belonging to our citizens are not considered subjects of exchange." As for easing the nation toward reconciliation by beseeching his fellow Southerners not to rise up in the wake of defeat, Lee did so only, according to Grant, in a manner "so grudging and pernicious in its effects as to be hardly realized."

Lee survived the war by five years, serving much of that time as president of Washington College, later renamed Washington and Lee University. His actions once again belie the myth. Lee is on record as urging his fellow Virginians to hire only whites. In denouncing federal attempts to impose racial equality on the South, he argued against Black suffrage, on the grounds that no former slave could possibly vote intelligently. As college president, he stood aside as the campus established a chapter of the Ku Klux Klan, soon renowned for kidnapping and raping Black girls from nearby missionary schools. When white students twice rallied, ready to lynch innocent Black men on college grounds, Lee and his administration did not interfere.

Robert E. Lee was, in fact, a white supremacist to his core. As a general, he earned and certainly deserved the reverence of his soldiers, but as a man, he left a legacy soiled by both his actions after the war and the inconvenient truth that he had led an insurrection against a government dedicated to liberation and freedom for all. And he did so in the name of slavery.

As the promises of Reconstruction grew fainter with each passing year, bigotry, hatred, and fear became ever more deeply entrenched, with legislatures throughout the South passing laws that separated Blacks from whites in every public space: churches and town squares, baseball diamonds and beaches. Named after a caricature, a Black minstrel from the stage, Jim Crow laws codified segregation, a cruel and unnatural perversion that was embraced as if a biblical admonition.

The immediate goal was to disenfranchise Blacks and take back any political or economic gains they had made after the war. The longer view envisioned the distinct possibility that having lost the war, the South might win the peace, even while avenging its own humiliation by condemning African Americans to the margins of American life. In 1881, Tennessee insisted that Blacks sit apart from whites in railroad cars; a decade later, Georgia expanded the law to include any form of transportation. Post offices and banks soon had separate windows; playgrounds, separate water fountains and swings; courthouses, separate Bibles. Cities passed zoning laws banning Blacks from entire neighborhoods. Small businesses earned the right to refuse service to people of color. In Alabama, it became a crime for a Black child to play checkers with a white child in a public park.

In 1892, a New Orleans shoemaker, Homer Plessy, who looked white but by racial law was said to be Black, challenged the authorities by taking a seat in a railroad car reserved for whites, much as Rosa Parks would do on a bus in Montgomery in 1955. Plessy, like Parks, would be arrested, but his criminal sentence would be upheld in an egregious Supreme Court decision that argued that separate facilities did not imply unequal facilities, thus denying that Plessy's rights had been violated in any way. Separate but equal, a rhetorical sleight of hand utterly removed from reality, would go unchallenged for seventy years.

Plessy v. Ferguson marked another low point in the history of the U.S. Supreme Court. Not only did the 1896 ruling preclude legal challenges to segregation, it also signaled the complete retreat of the federal government, virtually inviting retribution, as if announcing open season on Black people throughout the South. Several years later, the governor of Mississippi proclaimed with quiet confidence and no fear of sanction that "if it is necessary, every Negro in the state will be lynched."

Outside Atlanta, a farm worker, Sam Hose, was killed, cut up, and barbecued, his body parts sold as souvenirs. The Tulsa race massacre, which in 1921 destroyed the wealthiest Black community in the United States, started with a lynch mob. Every four days on average, somewhere in America, a Black man was hanged or burned alive. Altogether, between 1882 and 1968, more than 3,400 men and women were tortured and lynched, their limp and broken bodies left to swing "in the Southern breeze," as Billie Holiday would sing. "Strange fruit hangin' from the poplar trees."

IN 1913, THE SAME YEAR that Woodrow Wilson imposed segregation on all departments of the federal government, he traveled to Gettysburg to commemorate the fiftieth anniversary of the battle that more than any other had determined the outcome of the Civil War. As two small armies of old men, dressed in blue and gray, merged into one, Wilson proclaimed, "We have found one another again as brothers and comrades in arms, enemies no longer, generous friends rather, our battles long past, the quarrel forgotten." All around them, on both sides of the battlefield, scores of monuments had sprouted from the Pennsylvania earth, bronze and marble testaments that in their numbers invoked the scale of the forces that had clashed over three fateful days in that distant summer of 1863. Hovering over the ceremony was the spirit of reconciliation and a comfortable consensus that the war had been a struggle over the destiny of the nation, the rights of states versus the power of a federal government, a crucible from which the country had emerged as a more perfect union, ready to take on what would become the American Century. There was no talk of slavery, nor was a single Black veteran invited to attend.

Just four years later, Wilson would lead the country into a new and even more terrible war. More than 350,000 African Americans would serve, all in segregated units. Nearly two hundred would be awarded the French Legion of Honour. In 1917, the year America entered the war, thirty Black men were lynched. The year after the armistice, as the troops came home, seventy-six were strung up by white mobs, including ten veterans still dressed in their military uniforms. In 1920, a revitalized KKK boasted a membership of five million, a formidable force with a list of enemies and demons that had grown to include Jews and Catholics, immigrants and strangers. Five years later, Earl Little, a Baptist minister, and his wife, Louise, were living in Omaha, Nebraska, where Louise had just given birth to a son, Malcolm. They were alone, mother and infant, when the Klan arrived, threatening to lynch her husband. The family fled to Michigan, where within months a mob torched their home. Earl was killed by a streetcar, a suspicious death later confirmed as a homicide.

The life insurance company refused to pay out, leaving his widow penniless. The family survived on greens, mostly dandelions and weeds. In 1934, even as Louise struggled, fifteen African Americans were lynched, including Claude Neal, who was dragged from an Alabama jail and taken to Florida, where he was tortured and hanged before a cheering mob of four thousand.

In the U.S. Senate, Southern politicians actively opposed a bill that called for an end to lynching. Politics was, at any rate, beyond the reach of African Americans; in 1936, less than 4 percent were registered to vote. With eight children to support, Louise Little broke, and in 1939 she was sent to an asylum. Her son Malcolm ended up in foster care and then a home for delinquents, the first of a revolving series of institutional doors that ultimately led to prison, where he found his salvation in religion. He changed his name to Malcolm X.

America returned to war in 1941. More than 1.2 million African Americans enlisted, only to be relegated to menial duties, servicing the front. None were permitted to join either the Army Air Forces or the Marine Corps. In the factories, they were segregated from whites. In Detroit, barricades on the streets kept Black families from moving into public housing projects. A billboard read, "We want white tenants in our white community." In Virginia, two Black Army sergeants refused to give up their seats on a bus. Both were beaten and jailed, as was an Army nurse in Alabama, her nose broken by a policeman when she refused to move to the back of the bus. Charles Drew, then head of the Red Cross Blood Bank, found a way to preserve blood, an innovation that would save thousands of soldiers, white and Black, wounded in battle. The Red Cross heralded his discovery but refused to treat white patients with blood donated by African Americans, for fear of racial mixing by transfusion. Drew, who was Black, resigned in protest.

The humiliation knew no bounds. When the war ended, Black men who had fought and watched their brothers die were banned from the American Legion and excluded from the GI Bill, which provided every white veteran with a free college education. In 1946, a veteran was lynched in Georgia; a year later, another in Louisiana.

As late as 1950, fully 80 percent of African Americans in the South had no way to vote. Activists led by Thurgood Marshall turned to the courts. In 1954, in a seminal ruling, *Brown v. Board of Education*, the chief justice, Earl Warren, determined that "separate educational facilities are inherently unequal." This single phrase broke the back of segregation.

The South responded with death threats and calls for Warren's impeachment. Governor George Wallace offered to block the doors of the University of Alabama with his own body rather than allow any Black student access to an integrated education. Having lost a previous election, he vowed that "no other son of a bitch will ever out-ni— me again." In 1962, with the help of a speech writer recruited from the Klan, Wallace won 96 percent of the vote. In his inaugural address, he invoked Jefferson Davis and proclaimed, "Segregation now, segregation tomorrow, segregation forever." Faced with court action that ordered the integration of public swimming pools, the city of Montgomery drained the pools and shut down the facilities.

The fight moved from the courts into the streets, with the Montgomery bus boycott, the first sit-ins, and the radiant oratory of Martin Luther King Jr. Television brought to the conscience of a nation horrific images of dogs being unleashed on peaceful protesters, children being beaten at the doorways to schools, a bus in a torch of flames as a mob screamed hysterically, "Let's burn them alive." Alabama's governor, John Patterson, told one of Robert Kennedy's aides, "There's nobody in the whole country that's got the spine to stand up to the goddamned ni—s except me."

The optics were not good, neither at home nor abroad. It was the height of the Cold War. America advertised itself as the bastion of freedom. Yet when the finance minister of Ghana dropped by a Howard Johnson's in Delaware to order an orange juice, he was denied service. The Haitian minister of agriculture, invited to Mississippi to attend a conference, was not permitted to stay in the host hotel. Racial discrimination, acknowledged Dean Acheson, the secretary of state, challenged the country's ability to lay moral claim to the leadership of the democratic world.

In June 1963, John Kennedy addressed the nation and told the truth:

> When Americans are sent to Viet-Nam or West Berlin, we do not ask for whites only... If an American, because his skin is dark, cannot eat lunch in a restaurant open to the public, if he cannot send his children to the best public school available, if he cannot vote for the public officials who will represent him, if, in short, he cannot enjoy the full and free life which all of us want, then who among us would be content to have the color of his skin changed and stand in his place?

Two months later, some 250,000 marched on Washington in support of civil rights, then the largest demonstration ever to gather on the National Mall. As King rose to the podium,

Kennedy was listening. Moved by the multitudes, the Baptist minister tossed aside his prepared remarks and spoke as a prophet, sharing a dream of redemption and hope that would resonate through history. It was the first time the president had heard a complete speech from King. Words soared as if sounding the very bells of freedom. Everything changed. Kennedy was moved to act. But within three months, he would be dead, shot down by a white assassin.

Malcolm X rejected King's call for nonviolence, the tactics of sit-ins and peaceful protest. "Anybody can sit," he declared. "It takes a man to stand." In just over a year, he, too, would be dead, his body riddled by twenty-one bullets, including fifteen fired at point-blank range.

Fourteen days after the assassination of Malcolm X, John Lewis and several hundred marchers approached the Alabama River in Selma, on their way to Montgomery. Ahead of them was the Edmund Pettus Bridge, named for a Confederate general and KKK leader. At the time, Blacks were a third of Selma's population but just 1 percent of registered voters. As the protesters crossed the bridge, they were assaulted by five hundred state troopers, some mounted on horses, others with dogs. The entire country watched on live television and bore witness to an onslaught that would become known as Bloody Sunday. In Washington, Lyndon Johnson leveraged the outrage to secure passage of the Voting Rights Act, which became law on August 6, 1965. Five days later, riots erupted in Watts, in South Central Los Angeles. Martin Luther King Jr. flew to California and called for calm, but no one listened. The state mobilized a small army—fourteen thousand members of the National Guard—to quell the unrest.

For the next four summers, the nation went to war with itself. Urban riots, invariably sparked by police violence, left inner cities aflame. On television, it was difficult to distinguish the chaos and looting and explosions in Newark and Detroit from the reports being broadcast from the crumbling cities under siege in Vietnam. In the Black neighborhoods of Detroit, more than seven thousand African Americans were arrested, even as some two thousand buildings went up in smoke. To restore order, the government sent in 9,600 paratroopers of the 101st and 82nd Airborne Divisions. Some of the same soldiers who were deployed to Detroit would later serve in Vietnam, where African Americans, though a tenth of the national population, made up a quarter of the military force, with some airborne combat units being majority Black. Many of those charged with arresting and, if necessary, shooting young Black men in Detroit were themselves Black and destined to die months later in a pointless frontal assault at Hamburger Hill, an isolated jungle ridge with no strategic value, abandoned by the Americans within a fortnight of its capture.

As images of Vietnam came home, along with coffins, those in the inner cities turned to violence. In Newark, a city that was 65 percent Black, eighteen babies died of diarrhea in a single year in a hospital infested with bats. In Watts, where 35,000 took to the streets, there was no hospital. In 1967, the year Detroit burned, thirty Black Panthers armed with pistols and shotguns entered the California State Capitol in Sacramento during a debate on gun control. Opposing the measure, Bobby Seale invoked the Second Amendment with a rationale that most certainly was not on the mind of James Madison when he drafted the Bill of Rights. "Black people,"

Seale declared, "have begged, prayed, petitioned, demonstrated, and everything else to get the racist power structure of America to right the wrongs which have historically been perpetuated against black people... the time has come for black people to arm themselves against this terror before it is too late." Through the long lens of American history, this statement reads as a reasonable and truthful observation, save perhaps for the last line. But for those in the comfortable suburbs, they were the words of a terrorist, and a Black one at that.

In April 1967, Martin Luther King Jr. broke with Lyndon Johnson and came out against the Vietnam War, ending a complicated dynamic that had made possible both the Civil Rights Act of 1964 and the Voting Rights Act of 1965. Fatally weakened by the war, the president stunned the country a year later when he announced that he would not seek re-election and would instead dedicate his remaining months in office to finding a way to end the conflict. Four days later, King was cut down by an assassin's bullet in Memphis. The killer was an ex-con, an avowed segregationist, and an avid supporter of the presidential candidate George Wallace. The Black activist Stokely Carmichael described King's murder as an act of war and encouraged anyone who would listen to go home and get their guns.

In Indianapolis, word of the assassination reached Robert Kennedy just as he was about to address a large African American audience. The news rolled like a dark wave over the adoring crowd, ecstatic in one moment, crushed with grief in the next. From the back of a flatbed truck, the former attorney general and Democratic candidate for president said that he knew what it was like to lose a brother. He urged everyone to go home in peace and pray for the King family. Then, from memory, he recited lines from Aeschylus: "Even in our sleep, pain which cannot forget falls drop by drop upon the heart, until, in our own despair, against our will, comes wisdom through the awful grace of God."

That night, Indianapolis was the only major American city that did not burn. Two months later, Bobby Kennedy, having won the California primary with a clear path to the White House, was shot dead as he left the stage of his victory celebration at the Ambassador Hotel.

THE COUNTRY CLEAVED IN AGONY. The endless war, the cities on fire, children in every home growing up to the annual rhythm of assassinations, their older siblings taking to the streets, taking drugs, turning on their parents, their country, their world. Social movements capitalized on the turmoil. Women mobilized, demanding their share of economic and political power and, above all, control of their own bodies. Gay men and women began their long march to sexual freedom and marriage equality. Though inspiring to some, such transformations inevitably proved unsettling to most—those who still lived by simple truths and loyalties: family, God, country.

Rising from the ashes of his own despair, the shadow of his failures, Richard Nixon took hold of this fear and turned it into a political movement. Here was a politician who understood the potential of fear, the power of hate. Mobilizing uncertainty, he heralded the silent majority—an invention that he defined as the real citizens, implying that anyone living outside the norm was deviant. Though caring little about drug use, as John Ehrlichman, his closest domestic adviser, later acknowledged, Nixon in 1971 set in motion the War on Drugs, strictly as a political ploy. The goal was to galvanize his base, using hippies, Blacks, students, and anyone against the war as foils, playing a new and expanded card that went beyond race. Nixon was a master at poisoning the hearts of his followers. Communism, drugs, and the Devil grew into one great demonic threat. A trillion dollars would be spent, and fifty years on there would be more people misusing drugs than at any time since the beginning of Nixon's misguided crusade.

The greatest folly in the history of public policy would leave the United States the only developed country where there are more citizens with criminal records than with university degrees. By 2018, African Americans, just 13 percent of the population, filled 34 percent of prison cells, in good measure because white politicians had made sanctions for possession of crack cocaine a hundred times more severe than for powdered cocaine. Pharmacologically, they are two forms of the same drug. One is smoked, the other snorted. The only other difference is marketing. Crack sells at a per-unit price that puts it within reach of those living in the streets; cocaine retails by the gram at prices most affordable to those in boardrooms.

Then, in the seesaw of hope and despair that is America, Barack Obama, son of a Black father and a white mother, grandson of Africa and scion of Harvard, with a gift for oratory and a profound understanding of what words can do, rekindled the nation's better dreams and reached the White House.

In New York, Donald Trump began his own foray into politics with slander, floating the lie that Obama was born in Kenya and thus disqualified from serving as president. Trump had the resources, instincts, and personality to turn defamation into conspiracy, single-handedly fueling a cult belief in "birtherism" as he toyed with fantasies about his political future.

Trump inherited both his values and his money from his father, Fred, a landlord to the middle class, who instructed his son to mark housing applications from African Americans with a C, for colored, as a way of excluding them from any Trump property. Donald's older brother, rejected by their father as being too soft, turned to drink; he had dreamt of becoming a pilot. Donald, in contrast, became his father's image. As a casino owner, he would order his managers to remove any Black guests from the floor when he and his wife wanted to play the slots.

In 1989, when five young men of color were accused of raping a white woman in Central Park, Trump took out full-page ads in the New York tabloids to call for their executions. Twelve years later, new evidence proved their innocence. The courts awarded $41 million as compensation for their false convictions, which the plaintiffs claimed was little more than a "racially motivated conspiracy." Trump once again took to the newspapers, insisting without evidence that the so-called Central Park Five remained guilty. He published their names, phone numbers, and addresses, as if inviting mob violence. Lawyers close to the case compared Trump's actions to a call for lynching.

In the Oval Office, Trump referred to African countries as "shithole" nations, noting that immigrants from places like Nigeria, having experienced America, would never want to "go back to their huts." In his first year as president, hurricanes of equal force devastated Texas and Puerto Rico; in nine days, Trump dispatched three times the workforce and twenty-three times the relief money to Houston, leaving Puerto Rico in the dark.

In February 2017, the city council in Charlottesville, Virginia, voted to remove a statue of Robert E. Lee. Six months later, a mob of neo-Nazis and heavily armed militia members rallied to hear, among other speakers, David Duke, the former head of the Ku Klux Klan. They marched through the night with torches aflame, shouting the very slogans of Hitler's brownshirts: "Jews will not replace us!" "Blood and soil!" A young Black man, DeAndre Harris, was beaten by six thugs. A 32-year-old white woman, Heather Heyer, was killed and thirty-five others injured when an avowed white supremacist drove his vehicle into a crowd of counterprotesters. Two days later, with the country in shock, Trump remarked that there had been "blame on both sides... You had some very bad people in that group, but you also had people that were very fine people, on both sides."

In truth, what Charlottesville revealed was white nationalism on the march, in the open, without shame, as infused with righteous certainty as were the secessionists of the Confederacy, the lynch mobs of Tennessee. United by nostalgia, wistful for a lost age of white Christian power, with a profound sense of victimization, believing that the truth was whatever they wished it to be, they marched with eyes wide open, infused with fury.

ON JANUARY 6, 2021, several thousand like-minded patriots, incited directly by Donald Trump, stormed the Capitol in Washington and openly violated the heart of American democracy. En route, they paused to pray under banners that declared "Jesus is my savior. Trump is my president." None would admit that Trump had been decisively defeated at the polls.

As they marched up Pennsylvania Avenue, they beseeched God to bring an end to the "evil of Congress." They pushed past the Capitol police, breaking through doors and windows, trashing offices, and smashing furniture. A woman was shot and killed, another trampled by the mob. An officer died, his head crushed with a fire extinguisher. Another was dragged down a set of stairs and beaten with a pole wrapped in an American flag. Altogether, fifty officers were injured and fifteen hospitalized. There was feverish talk of coups and sedition and the overthrow of democracy. But at the end of the day, only one shot was fired—the bullet that killed Ashli Babbitt. Once the building was breached, the Trumpers for the most part appeared to be uncertain of what to do. They wandered the corridors, milled about in the halls, gathered beneath the vaulted arches and domes of a building that many had seen only on television. Mostly, they photographed themselves. If this was a coup d'état, it was revolution as a selfie, the American state assaulted by iPhones.

What was most haunting was not what the trespassers did but how they were treated. On video the police can be seen chatting them up, not unlike security crews at a rock concert confronting a raucous audience. There was pushing and shoving, but no one was beaten, dragged by the hair, sprayed with mace, or pounded unconscious. Such treatment, apparently, was reserved for those protesting in favor of racial justice, such as the young men and women, white and Black, who had marched in the streets of the capital the previous summer. One can only imagine what their fate would have been had they stormed the halls of Congress and violated the inner sanctum of political power.

On the night of the attack, eight Republican senators and 137 representatives, many of whom had been seen on camera earlier in the day cowering in fear of Trump's mob, voted in support of spurious accusations of voter fraud, in lockstep with a president who had just instigated an assault on the very symbol of American democracy.

Defeated at the polls, the Republicans turned their focus to voter suppression, imposing new barriers to casting votes, gerrymandering congressional districts, outlawing private donations that provide resources to oversee the fair administration of elections, doing whatever they could to impede turnout in future elections in predominantly Black and Hispanic Democratic strongholds. In Georgia, this included a push to limit early voting on Sundays, eliminating a long tradition of African Americans heading to the polls after church. No tactic was too callous or too trivial.

The motivation is clear. In a manner that goes beyond any one candidate or any election cycle, the party of Abraham Lincoln has become the party of white grievance, clinging to power by invoking a darkness that has always existed in the American reality. What long lay hidden, at least in polite society, Trump's rhetoric made fashionable, shattering the boundaries of discretion and decorum in the flaunting of prejudice and bigotry.

Perhaps the demographics made it inevitable. The white majority will soon become a minority. For many Americans, as history attests, this presents an existential challenge. What becomes of white Americans when their country is no longer majority white? What becomes of Christianity when its most vocal practitioners remain deaf to Christ's call for charity and mercy for all? And what of his warning in the book of Matthew that those who turn their backs on the stranger and deny help to the needy will be banished from his side and cast "cursed into the eternal fire prepared for the devil and his angels"? Surely no spiritual text has ever been more selectively read than the New Testament in the hands of white evangelicals of the political right.

"NOT EVERYTHING THAT IS FACED CAN BE CHANGED," James Baldwin wrote decades ago, "but nothing can be changed until it is faced." What, indeed, becomes of America when it faces the mirror of its exceptionalism only to see glass shards scattered on the rotunda floor? The four dark years of the Trump presidency were not anomalous; they were consistent with all that has transpired over a long history. The anger, the racial hatred, the scapegoating, the violence, the lies and delusions, the rhetoric and bullying, the fundamental weakness on display, all the contradictions—it is as if nothing has been learned, nothing has been resolved, and the structural divide between Black and white remains as wide as the chasm between a nation's foundational myths and its reality.

George Floyd, in Minneapolis, was just one more body piled upon the heaps of dead, the tens of thousands of victims of America's original sin. His final words were the last gasp of a nation that has never come clean about its past, that is no longer able to breathe, that may never be able to breathe unless it comes to another great and transcendent reckoning, a cleansing of the national soul, a purification that all the fires of all the wars have not yet managed to achieve. Floyd's killer was found guilty, and perhaps that's a step toward justice. But since Floyd's death on May 25, 2020, nearly seven hundred Black men and women have died as a result of police violence. The data tell the story. This is America as it is and has always been.

James Baldwin also saw reason for hope all those years ago. "To accept one's past—one's history—is not the same thing as drowning in it," he wrote. "It is learning how to use it. An invented past can never be used; it cracks and crumbles under the pressures of life like clay in a season of drought." And then he added perhaps the most promising words of all, words that could serve as a charter for a nation that, at long last, aspires to become the country it has long purported to be:

> If we—and now I mean the relatively conscious whites and the relatively conscious blacks, who must, like lovers, insist on, or create the consciousness of the others—do not falter in our duty now, we may be able, handful that we are, to end the racial nightmare, and achieve our country, and change the history of the world.

Perhaps one day words such as these will be inscribed in gleaming white marble on the National Mall. Those of Martin Luther King Jr. are already there, etched on a memorial the very idea of which would have been unimaginable in his lifetime. It is here that my modest tours of Washington now end, in a sea of Americans of every creed and color who have made it one of the most visited sites in the city, surpassing in popularity those dedicated to Jefferson and Washington. "Darkness cannot drive out darkness," the words read, "only light can do that."

King opposed both racism and the system that produced the racist. And though three out of every four Americans disapproved of him at the time of his death, he believed that redemption was possible, that people tortured by sin and hatred could be turned to the light, that even the most vile could lay down their burden of bias and bigotry. "We shall overcome," his words on the National Mall continue, "because the arc of the moral universe is long, but it bends toward justice." Here surely is the promise of America, a potent yet imperfect place, with a story that, mercifully, is still being written.

2

WHY
ANTHROPOLOGY MATTERS

IN 2012, both *Kiplinger* and *Forbes* ranked anthropology as
the least valuable undergraduate major, unleashing a small
wave of indignation as many outside the field rushed to
defend the study of culture as ideal preparation for any life
or career in an interconnected and globalized world. The
response from professional anthropologists, confronted by
both an existential challenge and public humiliation, was earnest but largely ineffective, for the voice of the discipline had
been muted by a generation of self-absorption, tempered by a
disregard for popular engagement that borders on contempt.

Ruth Benedict, acolyte of the great Franz Boas and in
1947 president of the American Anthropological Association
(AAA), reputedly said that the very purpose of anthropology
was to make the world safe for human differences.

Today, such activism seems as passé as a pith helmet. In
the immediate aftermath of 9/11, the AAA met in Washington, D.C. Four thousand anthropologists were in the nation's
capital in the wake of the biggest story of culture they or the
country would ever encounter. The entire gathering earned
but a mention in the *Washington Post*, a few lines in the gos-
sip section essentially noting that the nutcases were back in

town. It was hard to know who was more remiss, the government for failing to listen to the one profession that could have answered the question *Why do they hate us?* or the profession itself for failing to bring its considerable insights to the attention of the nation.

Perhaps fittingly it took an outsider to remind anthropologists why anthropology matters. Charles King, professor of international affairs at Georgetown University, begins his remarkable book *The Reinvention of Humanity* by asking us to envision the world as it existed in the minds of our grandparents, perhaps your great-grandparents. Race, he notes, was accepted as a given, a biological fact, with lineages dividing white from Black reaching back through primordial time. Differences in customs and beliefs reflected differences in intelligence and destiny, with every culture finding its rung on an evolutionary ladder rising from the savage to the barbarian to the civilized of the Strand in London, with technological wizardry, the great achievement of the West, being the sole measure of progress and success.

Sexual and behavioral characteristics were presumed to be fixed. Whites were smart and industrious, Blacks physically strong but lazy, and some people were barely distinguishable from animals; as late as 1902, it was debated in parliament in Australia whether Aboriginal people were human beings. Politics was the domain of men, charity work and the home the realm of women. Women's suffrage in America only came in 1920. Immigrants were seen as a threat, even by those who had themselves only just managed to claw their way ashore. The poor were responsible for their own miseries, even as the British Army reported that the height of officers recruited in 1914 was on average six inches taller than that of enlisted men, simply because of nutrition. As for the blind, deaf, and dumb, the cripples, morons, mongoloids, and the mad, they were best locked away, lobotomized, and even killed to remove them from the gene pool.

The superiority of the white man was accepted with such assurance that the *Oxford English Dictionary* in 1911 had no entries for racism or colonialism. As recently as 1965, Carleton Coon completed a set of two books, *The Origin of Races* and *The Living Races of Man*, in which he advanced the theory that the political and technological dominance of Europeans was a natural consequence of their evolved genetic superiority. He even asserted that "racial intermixture can upset the genetic as well as the social equilibrium of a group." Coon, at the time of his retirement in 1963, was a respected professor and curator at the University of Pennsylvania. Interracial marriage remained illegal across much of the United States until 1967.

Today, not two generations on, it goes without saying that no educated person would share any of these bankrupt certitudes. By the same token, what we take for granted would be unimaginable to those who fiercely defended convictions that appear to the modern eye both transparently wrong and morally reprehensible. All of which raises a question. What was it that allowed for such a transformation, causing our culture to change so dramatically in so little time?

Political movements are built upon the possibility of change, possibilities brought into being by new ways of thinking. Before any of these struggles could flourish, something fundamental, some flash of insight, had to challenge and, in time, shatter the intellectual foundations that supported archaic beliefs as irrelevant to our lives today as the notions of nineteenth-century clergymen, certain that the Earth was but six thousand years old.

The catalyst, as Charles King reminds us, was the wisdom and scientific genius of Franz Boas and a small band of courageous scholars—Margaret Mead, Alfred Kroeber, Elsie Clews Parsons, Melville Herskovits, Edward Sapir, Robert Lowie, Ruth Benedict, Zora Neale Hurston, and many others—contrarians all, who came into his orbit, destined to change the world. We live today in the social landscape of their dreams. If you find it normal, for example, that an Irish boy would have an Asian girlfriend, or that a Jewish friend might find solace in the Buddhist dharma, or that a person born with a male body could self-identify as a woman, then you are a child of anthropology.

If you recognize that marriage need not exclusively imply a man and a woman, that single mothers can be good mothers, and that two men or two women can raise good families as long as there is love in the home, it's because you've embraced values and intuitions inconceivable to your great-grandparents. And if you believe that wisdom may be found in all spiritual traditions, that people in all places are always dancing with new possibilities for life, that one preserves jam but not culture, then you share a vision of compassion and inclusion that is perhaps the most sublime revelation of our species, the scientific realization that all of humanity is one interconnected and undivided whole.

Widely acknowledged as the father of American cultural anthropology, Franz Boas was the first scholar to explore in a truly open and neutral manner how human social perceptions are formed, and how members of distinct societies become conditioned to see and interpret the world. What, he asked, was the nature of knowing? Who decided what was to be known? How do seemingly random beliefs and convictions converge into this thing called *culture*, a term that he was the first to promote as an organizing principle, a useful point of intellectual departure.

Far ahead of his time, Boas recognized that every distinct social community, every cluster of people distinguished by language or adaptive inclination, was a unique facet of the human legacy and its promise. Each was a product of its own history. None existed in an absolute sense; every culture was but a model of reality. We create our social realms, Boas would say, determine what we then define as being common sense, universal truths, the appropriate rules and codes of behavior. Beauty really does lie in the eye of the beholder. Manners don't make the man; people invent the manners. Race is a cultural construct, derived not from biology but born in the realm of ideas.

Critically, none of this implied an extreme relativism, as if every human behavior must be accepted simply because it exists. Boas never called for the elimination of judgment, only for its suspension so that the very judgments we are ethically and morally obliged to make as human beings may be informed ones. Even as he graced the cover of *Time* magazine in 1936, a German Jew in exile from a homeland already dripping in blood, Boas railed against the cruel conceits and stupidity of scientific racism. Inspired by his time among the Inuit on Baffin Island, and later among the Kwakwaka'wakw in the salmon forests of the Pacific Northwest, he informed all who would listen that the other peoples of the world were not failed attempts to be them, failed attempts to be modern. Every culture was a unique expression of the human imagination and heart. Each was a unique answer to a fundamental question: What does it mean to be human and alive? When asked that question, humanity responds in seven thousand different languages, voices that collectively comprise our repertoire for dealing with all the challenges that will confront us as a species.

Boas would not live to see his insights and intuitions confirmed by hard science, let alone define the zeitgeist of a new global culture. But, eighty years on, studies of the human genome have indeed revealed the genetic endowment of humanity to be a single continuum. Race truly is a fiction. We are all cut from the same genetic cloth, all descendants of common ancestors, including those who walked out of Africa some 65,000 years ago, embarking on a journey that over 40,000 years, a mere 2,500 generations, carried the human spirit to every corner of the habitable world.

But here is the important idea. If we are all cut from the same fabric of life, then by definition we all share the same mental acuity, the same raw genius. Whether this intellectual potential is exercised through technological innovation or through the untangling of complex threads of memory inherent in a myth is simply a matter of choice and orientation, adaptive insights and cultural emphasis. There is no hierarchy of progress in the history of culture, no evolutionary ladder to success.

Boas and his students were right. The brilliance of scientific research, the revelations of modern genetics, has affirmed in an astonishing way both the unity of humanity and the essential wisdom of cultural relativism. Every culture really does have something to say; each deserves to be heard, just as none has a monopoly on the route to the divine.

As a scholar, Boas ranks with Einstein, Darwin, and Freud as one of the four intellectual pillars of modernity. His core idea, distilled in the notion of cultural relativism, was a radical departure, as unique in its way as was Einstein's theory of relativity in the discipline of physics. Everything Boas proposed ran against orthodoxy. It was a shattering of the European mind, the sociological equivalent of the splitting of the atom. And though his research took him to esoteric realms of myth and shamanism, symbolism and the spirit, he remained grounded in the politics of racial and economic justice, the promise and potential of social change. A tireless campaigner for human rights, Boas maintained always that anthropology as a science only made sense if it was practiced in the service of a higher tolerance. "It is possible," wrote Thomas Gossett in his 1963 book *Race: The History of an Idea in America*, that "Boas did more to combat race prejudice than any other person in history."

Though remembered today as the giants of the discipline, Boas and his students in their time were dismissed from jobs because of their activism, denied promotion because of their beliefs, harassed by the FBI as the subversives they truly were, and attacked in the press just for being different. And yet they stood their ground, and because they did, as Charles King writes, "anthropology came into its own on the front lines of the great moral battle of our time ... [as it] anticipated and in good measure built the intellectual foundations for the seismic social changes of the last hundred years from women's suffrage and civil rights to sexual revolution and marriage equality."

Were Boas to be with us today, his voice would surely resound in the public square, the media, in all the halls of power. He would never sit back in silence as fully half the languages of the world hover on the brink of extinction, implying the loss within a single generation of half of humanity's intellectual, ecological, and spiritual legacy. To those who suggest that Indigenous cultures are destined to fade away, he would reply that change and technology pose no threat to culture, but power does. Cultures under threat are neither fragile nor vestigial; in every instance, they comprise vital and dynamic communities being driven out of existence by identifiable forces. If human beings are the agents of cultural loss, Boas would note, we can surely be facilitators of cultural survival.

Anthropology matters because it allows us to look beneath the surface of things. The very existence of other ways of being, other ways of thinking, other visions of life itself puts the lie to those in our own culture who say that we cannot change, as we know we must, the fundamental way in which we inhabit this planet. Anthropology is the antidote to nativism, the enemy of hate, a vaccine of understanding, tolerance, and compassion that silences the rhetoric of demagogues, inoculating the world against the likes of the Proud Boys and Donald Trump. As events over recent years have shown, the struggle long ago championed by Franz Boas continues to this day. Never has the voice of anthropology been more important.

But it must be spoken to be heard. With a million Uighurs in Chinese prison camps, the forests of the Penan in Sarawak laid waste, and the very homeland of the Inuit melting from beneath their lives, contemporary anthropologists must surely do better than indulging in doctrinal grievance studies, seminars on intersectionality, the use of pronouns, and other multiple expressions of woke orthodoxy, if the discipline is to avoid the indictment of actually being the most worthless of undergraduate degrees.

3

THE PROMISED LAND

FOR ALL OF ITS HISTORY, Jerusalem has been a spiritual locus of the world, the place where God resides. All three of the Abrahamic religions—Judaism, Christianity, and Islam— consider it a holy city. Some of the most sacred sites of all three religions are found in Jerusalem, and all three share and claim a single site, the Temple Mount, the axis mundi of the universe.

Jerusalem has been the ancestral and spiritual home of the Jewish people since the tenth century BCE. Three times a day, for thousands of years, Jewish prayers from around the world have been directed toward the city and the Temple Mount, whence they are said to ascend to heaven. The Talmud says: "If someone is praying outside the Land of Israel, he should direct his heart in the direction of Israel. When praying within Israel, direct the heart toward Jerusalem. Those in Jerusalem should direct their hearts to the Temple."

Jewish reverence for the city and the Temple Mount is rooted in biblical history. It was on this height of land that Abraham spoke to God and came close to sacrificing his son Isaac, before forging a covenant with God that secured the eternal life of the Jewish people. From here Jacob dreamed of the ladder ascending to heaven. When Solomon, son of David, completed the First Temple in 950 BCE, he beseeched God to heed the prayers of Jews and non-Jews alike, that the temple might be, in the words of the prophet Isaiah, "a house of prayer for all nations."

In 580 BCE, the Babylonians sacked Jerusalem, destroying the temple and sending the Jewish people into exile. But in time they returned and, on the same sacred site, built the Second Temple, which was dedicated in 516 BCE. Five hundred years later, Herod the Great massively expanded the size of the Temple Mount, enlarging the sacred structure and doubling the size of the platform upon which it stood. But Herod's Temple would not long endure. In 70 CE, even as their legions besieged Masada, brutally crushing the Jewish uprising, the Romans destroyed the temple, leaving only the remnants of the massive walls that had been built by Herod to support the expansion of the temple platform. These include the Western Wall so revered today.

For Christians, Jerusalem is where Jesus was brought as a child to attend festivals and be presented at temple. It is where he preached as a young man, worked miracles of healing, chased away the merchants who had defiled the sacred precincts. Jerusalem was the site of his "last supper," his arrest in the Garden of Gethsemane, his trial and crucifixion at Golgotha, his burial, resurrection, and final ascension to the side of God in heaven. The Church of the Holy Sepulchre covers the very ground where Jesus was crucified and laid in the tomb.

For Muslims, Jerusalem ranks behind only Mecca and Medina in spiritual significance, and in the early years of Islam, the faithful turned not to Mecca but to Jerusalem in prayer. Muhammad, born in 570 CE, is believed by the faithful to be but a messenger of God, the last of a long line of prophets that includes Abraham, David, Solomon, and Jesus, all of whom are mentioned and revered in the Qur'an, the holy book of the Islamic faith. Indeed, Islam was inspired by the same pantheon of biblical figures familiar to every Christian and Jew: Adam, Noah, Moses, Joshua, Samuel, Isaac, Jacob and his sons, John the Baptist, Lazarus, and many others. Abraham is the common ancestor and the ultimate progenitor of Arab, Christian, and Jew.

The Temple Mount also figures prominently in the story of Islam. According to the Qur'an, on a wondrous night in 610 CE, Muhammad, mounted on his miraculous horse al-Buraq, visited Jerusalem, where he prayed before ascending to heaven to receive from Allah the second pillar of Islam, the instructions to pray five times a day, a practice followed today by Muslims worldwide. The very spot where the Prophet ascended to heaven is now a sacred shrine, the Dome of the Rock, built in 691 CE on the Temple Mount some fifty years after the city came under Muslim rule. Where Muhammad tethered his horse before ascending to heaven is today the al-Buraq Mosque, just inside the wall at the south end of the Western Wall Plaza.

The Temple Mount covers roughly 140 acres. There is surely no other place in the world that resonates with such religious passion, that celebrates each day the promise of faith, only in a spiritual setting where bitterness and hatred lurk, and violence is constantly waiting to flare. This tension comes down to history, much of it derived from the fact that of these three so closely related Abrahamic traditions, two— Christianity and Islam—are the only evangelical religions that presume to have a monopoly on the path to the divine. Both have been prepared to seek converts through the power of the sword.

The Judaic tradition is quite the opposite. My first love in college was a beautiful Jewish American woman from Boston. We were together for almost four years, and I adored her family; her father was especially generous and welcoming. Yet the nearest her grandmother ever came to saying my name was "Annie, you don't want to live in Canada." It was inconceivable to her that her granddaughter might marry an outsider. Not that she was in any way unkind. Her reaction was rooted in her lived experience and her certain knowledge that solidarity had been for centuries the key to the cultural survival of the Jewish people. Their religious tradition does not include a mandate to persuade the rest of the world to embrace it. Jews have no interest in obliging the rest of humanity to think as they do. They simply want to be left alone to live.

The existential agony of the Jewish people originates both in the spasms of persecution that have marked all their history, culminating in the most hideous and savage act of the twentieth century, and in the insecurity and uncertainty certain to afflict any people cast adrift from their homeland for 1,900 years.

For Jews everywhere, the remnants of the temple, the Western Wall, have always been endowed with everlasting sanctity. Jerusalem itself has been destroyed nine times, but never the Wall, protected as it is by the wings of angels. Physically it is imposing, seemingly impregnable, 105 feet high, the exposed section standing 62 feet tall, 45 courses of stone, 28 above ground, 17 below, the largest of the stones weighing an astonishing 517 tons. Nothing can topple the Wall, and as the Jewish people water it with their tears and melt the stones with their kisses, they achieve spiritual clarity and purpose as God's eternal nation, as his Chosen People.

Palestinian Arabs naturally disagree. They claim the Wall as a part of the al-Aqsa Mosque and suggest that Jews did not consider it a place of worship until the late nineteenth century, when the Zionists began to dream of a national state. Others point to the sixteenth century as the first sign of Jewish reverence for the Wall; still others say it all began after the Balfour Declaration of 1917. In 1973, King Faisal of Saudi Arabia stated unequivocally, and falsely, that not a single stone in the Western Wall relates to any aspect of Jewish history.

Although Jews were banned from Jerusalem for centuries, they were, under the Christian emperor Constantine I, given permission once a year to enter the city and lament the loss of the temple at the Wall—hence the pejorative term *Wailing Wall*. And in the sixteenth century under the Ottoman ruler Suleiman, Jews received official permission to worship at the site.

But such gestures of grace and conciliation were limited and rare. For most of the last many centuries, Jewish access to the Wall has been severely restricted. Efforts by Zionist leaders to purchase the Wall outright in the 1920s were rejected. The 1948 war left Jordan in control of the Old City, and Jews were barred entry for nineteen years, effectively banning Jewish prayer at the Wall. It was not until 1967 that Israeli paratroopers seized the Old City; Jerusalem, along with the Western Wall, came under Jewish control for the first time in two thousand years.

Photographs of Israeli soldiers weeping and dancing at the Wall flashed around the world, inspiring tens of thousands in America and western Europe still living in the shadow of the Holocaust. But there was a disturbing side to the celebration. Within three days, the Israeli military had bulldozed the Moroccan Quarter adjacent to the Wall, destroying the Sheikh Eid Mosque, built over one of Jerusalem's oldest Islamic schools, and laying waste to the houses of 106 Arab families. Many refused to leave their homes, and the bulldozers toppled them anyway, in at least one instance with men, women, and children still inside.

SO HOW DO WE BEGIN to understand this conflict, which has raged for so many generations with no end in sight? On the eve of my first visit to Jerusalem, I turned to two Israeli writers, Meron Benvenisti, author of *Sacred Landscape: The Buried History of the Holy Land Since 1948*, and Ari Shavit, who wrote *My Promised Land: The Triumph and Tragedy of Israel*. Both books are rooted in extraordinary scholarship; each is insightful, honest, and mercifully free of polemics. That such publications, written by Israelis, sons of the Zionist dream, can be celebrated in Israel speaks to the very best of what the country aspires to be. Few of Israel's neighbors in the Middle East would be as tolerant of journalists intent on illuminating the dark shadows of their nation's past.

Before leaving Vancouver, I also asked a close friend of mine, Shefa Siegel, son of a rabbi, to explain the essence of Jewish notions of return and the meaning of the Zionist dream. Shefa's great-grandfather played a significant role in the debate in the 1930s as to whether Jews should seek a home in Palestine or establish autonomous regions in underpopulated British colonies in Africa and elsewhere. It was a debate his great-grandfather lost in the inner circles of the Zionist movement. This is what Shefa wrote:

> Through history, Jews have been associated with the book, the inference being that it is through the intellect that Jews preserve their contact with the old ways, but this is a mistake. The book and the intellect have always been ritualistic methods of staying connected to the Land, for this is how the indigenous homeland of the Jews is known—as simply "the Land"—as if there could be no other place on the earth capable of replacing the ancestral territory. It is the one and only, the one true love, and for the two-thousand-year history of exile, this land occupied the messianic imagination of Jews wherever they landed, from Calcutta to Cartagena and Casablanca to Caracas. Redemption would surely come in the form of a return to the Land, reuniting the scattered tribes in a great pilgrimage back to the sacred Mount Zion.

ULTIMATELY, THE CONFLICT between Palestinians and Israelis is not about religion. Scores of shared ritual practices recall the common origins of Islam and Judaism: the custom of removing shoes upon entry to a sacred place, the exclusion of menstruating women from temple and mosque, the obligation to wash before prayer, pilgrimages at set times, the offering of gifts and sacrifices, the cult of the holy at the summit of every high hill, reverence for saints, sacred trees, mountains, and springs. The battle that has raged in the Middle East for nearly a century is all about land, memory, and the power to control history. As much as a conflict between peoples, it is a clash between two completely distinct historical narratives.

In 1900, Palestine was a province of the Ottoman Empire, and the Jews who lived there were but 0.4 percent of the global Jewish population. Between 1903 and 1913, more than a million Jews fled eastern Europe; just 35,000 chose to go to Palestine. Most—those who wanted a life—went to America. Those few who imagined utopia went to the Promised Land. They arrived not as Europeans but as Europe's victims and as representatives of all the victims of centuries of antisemitic hatred and violence.

They brought from the diaspora a dream of a lost homeland and a yearning for its landscapes. But when they returned from their long exile, they encountered a foreign country, foreign people, threatening landscapes, and a Palestinian culture rooted in 1,900 years of occupation and history.

This was the reality that had to be swept aside if the dream, maintained through all the years of agony and torment, was to be realized. Fired by longing and desire, the immigrants saw the Palestinian presence on the land as but a veneer laid over the hidden world and landscape of their dreams.

They searched for signs of the ancient world of their imaginings. When what they found proved insufficient, they redrew maps to impose over the alien and threatening landscape of Palestine a new cartography of Zion. They then set out to reshape the landscape itself, again in accordance with their vision and dreams. Their goal was to populate the land with new generations of native Jews, sons and daughters not of the diaspora but of Israel.

If the Arabs were noticed at all, it was through a lens of modernity that viewed Palestinians as anthropological curiosities. The pastoral Bedouin were elevated as a sort of "noble savage," spirited, independent, and free, sons of the desert stuck in time, as if inhabiting the dusty pages of an ancient biblical text. Zionist contempt fell upon urban Arabs and especially the rural peasant farmers, those said to have ruined the land with their primitive farming techniques, overgrazing, overbreeding, petty feuds, and essential ignorance.

One of the foundational myths of the state of Israel is the conviction that Jewish settlers did not rob Palestinians of their land; they did battle with nature to redeem the land from desolation. The Arabs, with their picturesque villages and primitive customs, were just part of the landscape. Once the desert had been conquered, there would be room for everyone, including the Palestinians, as long as they remained docile, mere extras on the theatrical stage upon which the Zionist drama would unfold.

A desolate land in need of redemption settled by a broken people, victims of the greatest outrage in the history of humanity, was a powerful narrative. But one thing stood in the way: the inconvenient truth that in the 1,900 years of Jewish exile, Palestinians had found a home in the land of milk and honey, and they would not be readily erased from memory.

THE NOTION THAT PALESTINE was a barren land before the arrival of the Zionist waves of immigration is misleading, as is the suggestion that Arab farms were marginal when it came to production. In 1918, the year the British took over Palestine from the Turks, Jews made up 8 percent of the population, and they owned just 2.4 percent of the land. By 1947, at the end of the British mandate, the Jewish population had increased to 500,000, one-third of the total, but in rural Palestine, Arabs outnumbered Jews by a factor of five. Jewish land ownership had more than doubled, but it still remained less than 6 percent of the total land area of Palestine.

Agricultural production remained largely in the hands of the Arabs. In 1947, Arab citrus groves covered more land than those of the Jews, and Arabs were responsible for more than 98 percent of the production of olives and dates, 73 percent of the grapes, 77 percent of the fresh vegetables, 95 percent of the watermelons, 76 percent of the plums and apricots, 57 percent of the apples and pears, 53 percent of the bananas, and 57 percent of the milk.

Notwithstanding their demographic and economic dominance in rural Palestine, Arabs had for more than a decade grown wary of the Jewish influx. The breaking point had come in 1936. In the previous five years, the Jewish population in Palestine had more than doubled to 384,000. In the wake of Hitler's consolidation of power in Nazi Germany, the need for a Jewish homeland was self-evident, and increasingly Palestine appeared to be the place. Palestinians could see no end to the waves of Jewish refugees and settlers.

There had been skirmishes and riots before, but the spring of 1936 marked the beginning of an all-consuming conflict, as Palestinian mobs killed Jews, and after four months of Arab terror, Jews reciprocated in kind. During these months, ideals died and the collective psyche of the Jews was transformed. Zionism went from a state of utopian bliss to a state of dystopian conflict from which the region has yet to recover. In 1936, the 350,000 Jews living in Palestine became a community at war.

A year later, a British royal commission first proposed partition, with the understanding that Arabs would be forcibly removed from any lands allotted to the Jews. From this moment forward, removal of the Arabs became part of mainstream Zionist thinking. It was the end of innocence and moral inhibitions; all was a matter of survival.

The Arab Revolt flared through 1938, a dance of blood marked by atrocities committed by both sides. Arab political leaders throughout the region heralded attacks on innocent Jews. Zionist leaders by contrast and to their credit denounced attacks on innocent Arab families, but the attacks continued and the death toll of Arabs soared far higher than that of the Jews. The British suppressed the unrest with an iron fist, but terrorism did not abate.

The outbreak of Hitler's war distracted the British even as it increased tensions in Palestine. At the end of 1942, Anthony Eden acknowledged in Parliament that Nazi Germany was exterminating Jews as explicit national policy. That year, 2.7 million men, women, and children had been murdered. To the Jews in Palestine, the Arab threat was nothing compared with the specter of German armies at the gates of Cairo heading east and those in Russia about to break through to the Caucasus, coming south.

It was at this time that Masada rose from the mists of memory to take on new meaning and significance. No longer a historical legend, it became a symbol of the life and death struggle of the Jews. The Holocaust was a human catastrophe on a scale not seen since the Middle Ages. For the Jewish people, nothing like it had happened since the destruction of the Second Temple.

What becomes of the Zionist dream when the millions of Jewish men, women, and children that Zionism was established to save have been reduced to ashes in the death camps? In the face of such horrors, Zionism no longer has anything to do with greening the desert; it is all about the very existence of a Jewish people under siege who will never surrender.

The story of Masada was largely unknown, the ruins deserted for over a thousand years. The site is only two hundred feet above sea level, but because the Dead Sea is thirteen hundred feet below sea level, the mesa of Masada rises dramatically to fifteen hundred feet. To the west is the Judean Desert; to the south, Sodom; and to the north, Jericho. On a very clear day, Jerusalem may just be seen. The slopes are steep, almost vertical; the summit is flat and rhomboid, two thousand feet long and a thousand feet across at the widest place.

Though the summit was fortified as early as the second century BCE, it was not fully developed until the reign of King Herod, who, beginning in 36 BCE, surrounded the rock with a casement wall, raised a watchtower and barracks, built houses and warehouses, carved cisterns into the stone, and crowned it all with a magnificent palace.

When the Romans crushed the Great Jewish Revolt in 70 CE, conquering Jerusalem and destroying the temple, a small group of Jewish zealots clung to Masada. In 72 CE, the Tenth Roman Legion closed in, built eight camps around its base, and prepared for an assault in the spring of 73 CE. On the night before the attack, 960 men, women, and children of Masada took their own lives rather than succumb to Roman rule.

The first to identify the site in the modern era were two American travelers, Edward Robinson and Eli Smith, in 1838. In 1842, American missionary Samuel Wolcott and English painter William J. Tipping became the first on record to climb to the top. An archeological survey was not completed until 1932.

Masada only took on epic dimensions with the rise of the Zionist movement. Not until 1923 was the only historical source of the story of Masada—Flavius Josephus's *The Jewish War*, written in 75 CE—translated into Hebrew. Two years later, the Zionist historian Joseph Klausner wrote glowingly of the zealots of Masada. Two years after that Yitzhak Lamdan published his tragic poem, "Masada."

As Jewish nationalism was revived, Masada gradually came into memory, but slowly. Until the outbreak of Hitler's war, it remained largely unheralded. But in the wake of the Holocaust, Zionism had no illusions. It would be a struggle to the death, a struggle that needed a symbol, and that was Masada.

IN 1947, THE UNITED NATIONS called for the partition of Palestine, a proposal embraced by the Jews but rejected by the Arabs. Civil war between Arab and Jew raged from December of 1947 through May 1948. On the eve of the British departure, the Israeli nation was declared on May 14. The following day, the fledging state was invaded by the combined military strength of Egypt, Jordan, Iraq, Syria, and Lebanon.

A war of annihilation that turned "humans into beasts" lasted until July 1949, when Israel, at the cost of six thousand dead, emerged victorious, in control of fully 78 percent of Palestine, half again as much as it had been promised in the original partition proposal. Palestinian Arabs were left with nothing save the destruction of their society, the establishment of a Jewish state in their homeland, and the expulsion of 700,000 people from their homes.

In the wake of the Israeli victory, what had been a wartime exodus of Palestinians became an opportunity for ethnic cleansing. Israel's goal was to secure an absolute Jewish majority, settle Jewish refugees on the lands abandoned by the Arabs, and guarantee the internal security of the state. Prime Minister David Ben-Gurion determined that all Palestinians who had fled their homes, by choice or coercion, leaving behind possessions, fields, orchards, water wells, mosques, and graveyards, would not be permitted to return.

The army was given explicit orders to prevent the infiltration of Arabs back to their former homes and if necessary to kill to prevent them from reoccupying their farms and villages. Acts of brutality included summary executions, rape, looting and plundering, and even the blowing up of homes still occupied by families.

Of the hundreds of Arab villages of Palestine, fully two-thirds were destroyed, including eighty that were plowed under and completely obliterated. Fruit orchards and olive groves covering 250,000 acres were uprooted to create fields of fodder for cattle. By 1949, two-thirds of all acreage devoted to grain in Israel was land that in 1947 had been occupied by Arabs. Before the war, one-third of the Palestinian Arabs lived in sixteen cities and towns, with a vibrant middle class. At the end of the war, Arab urban life disappeared. As 700,000 Arabs lost their homes, a similar number of Jews immigrated to Israel.

In Israel, amnesia was embraced as state policy. The Palestinian past was forgotten, even as the horror of the Holocaust was left behind as the new nation launched into a radiant future. All that mattered was what lay ahead. A country rising as a phoenix from the ashes had no time for suffering, remorse, doubts, or sentimentality.

By the 1950s, Israel was a nation on steroids. GDP rose 165 percent in nine years. Industrial production in five years increased 180 percent. Twenty new cities came into being along with four hundred Jewish villages, built on the ruins of what had once been Arab communities. Hebrew, a liturgical language of scripture, was made the official language. To be a part of the new state, the entire population had to learn a new language. In 1956, Israel, a country with a population of but 1.8 million, set out to make a nuclear bomb and by 1965 had done so, becoming one of the leading military powers in the world.

Within a decade of its founding, Israel had expunged Palestine from its memory and its soul. Cartographers wiped maps clean of Palestinian names. The goal was to eradicate all record of what had occurred during the 1,900 years of the Jewish people's absence. It was not a show of contempt for the Arabic heritage; it was a declaration of war upon it.

In the late nineteenth century, when the British first mapped Palestine, they published some nine thousand Arab names, a tenth of which were of Hebrew-Aramaic origin, the remainder dating from the 1,400 years since the Arab Conquest in 638 CE. The poetic quality of these names reflected a subtle sensitivity to landscape and a deep knowledge of place, nature, and climate. Some names described the physical characteristics of a landmark. Others ascribed properties to a place. Hundreds were named for animals—lions and wolves, ravens, doves, jackals, and lizards. Many were named for legendary men and women of history, prophets and saints, heroes and warriors.

All these names, steeped in meaning, rooted in centuries of memory, were wiped away, along with the villages and towns, the olive orchards and the cypress groves, all paved over by the builders of a new Zion.

AMONG THOSE LIVING outside the cauldron of the Middle East, passionate for peace but less certain of the origins of the conflict, it is often asked why Palestinians remain so belligerent, standing in the way of reconciliation with their refusal to accept the obvious: Israel exists, and the Israelis have nowhere else to go. Though true, such realism does little to soften the memories of those who lived through events that unfolded only yesterday, in the lifetimes of their parents and grandparents. For Palestinians to accept Israel's existence is to acknowledge, in the words of one Arab scholar, quoted by the writer Fouad Ajami, "that it is acceptable for people to settle someone else's country, expel its inhabitants, and ensure by all means that they never return. And that to complain, or even remind the world of the historical facts, is to be labeled an extremist, as if it is quite impolite and unacceptable to mention things that everyone knows actually happened."

This leaves the Palestinians today not unlike the Zionists of old. As modern Israel drowns in a sea of consumerism, and privatization has turned over the landscape to secular commercial interests—California, if you will, surrounded by ayatollahs—the Palestinian bond with their lost and pillaged land has come to symbolize their entire nation. And for them, history, even recent history, has slipped into the realm of myth.

The landscape has endowed the Palestinians with a national identity. They have not cast their identity over it, as did the Jewish immigrants; they have long molded their identity from it. The collective memory of the stolen land, compounded by the hundreds of thousands of personal memories of loss, serves as the inspiration for eternal resistance, a lifetime of struggle in which the fight itself has taken on epic and transcendent significance. In one of the tragic ironies of history, Palestinian Arabs, in their passion and longing for their lost land, have become what the Zionists once were: stateless and disenfranchised, but also determined and patient—a people victimized by history, united in suffering and faith, and quite prepared to wait 1,900 years for justice to be done.

4

THE UNRAVELING
OF AMERICA

NEVER IN OUR LIVES have we experienced such a global phenomenon. For the first time in the history of the world, all of
humanity, informed by the unprecedented reach of digital
technology, has come together, focused on the same existential threat, consumed by the same fears and uncertainties,
eagerly anticipating the same as yet unrealized promises of
medical science.

In a single season, civilization has been brought low by a
microscopic parasite ten thousand times smaller than a grain
of salt. COVID-19 attacks our physical bodies but also the cultural foundations of our lives, the toolbox of community and
connectivity that is for the human what claws and teeth are
for the tiger.

Our interventions to date have largely focused on miti-
gating the rate of spread, flattening the curve of morbidity.
There is no treatment at hand and no certainty of a vaccine
on the near horizon. The fastest vaccine ever developed
was for mumps. It took four years. COVID-19 killed 100,000
Americans in four months. There is some evidence that natural infection may not imply immunity, leaving some to question how effective a vaccine will be, even assuming one can
be found. And it must be safe. If the global population is to

be immunized, lethal complications in just one person in a thousand would imply the death of millions.

Pandemics and plagues have a way of shifting the course of history, and not always in a manner immediately evident to the survivors. In the fourteenth century, the Black Death killed close to half of Europe's population. A scarcity of labor led to increased wages. Rising expectations culminated in the Peasants' Revolt of 1381, an inflection point that marked the beginning of the end of the feudal order that had dominated medieval Europe for a thousand years.

The COVID pandemic will be remembered as such a moment in history, a seminal event whose significance will unfold only in the wake of the crisis. It will mark this era much as the 1914 assassination of Archduke Ferdinand, the stock market crash of 1929, and the 1933 ascent of Adolf Hitler became benchmarks of the last century, all harbingers of greater and more consequential outcomes.

COVID's historic significance lies not in what it implies for our daily lives. Change, after all, is the one constant of culture. All peoples in all places at all times are always dancing with new possibilities for life. As companies eliminate or downsize central offices, and as employees work from home, restaurants close, shopping malls shutter, streaming brings entertainment and sporting events into the home, and airline travel becomes ever more difficult and miserable, people will adapt, as we've always done. Fluidity of memory and a capacity to forget is perhaps the most haunting trait of our species. As history confirms, it allows us to come to terms with any degree of social, moral, or environmental degradation.

To be sure, financial uncertainty will cast a long shadow. Hovering over the global economy for some time will be the sober realization that all the money in the hands of all the nations on Earth will never be enough to offset the losses sustained when an entire world ceases to function, with workers and businesses everywhere facing a choice between economic and biological survival.

Unsettling as these transitions and circumstances will be, short of a complete economic collapse, none stands out as a turning point in history. But what surely does is the absolutely devastating impact that the pandemic has had on the reputation and international standing of the United States of America.

In a dark season of pestilence, COVID has reduced to tatters the illusion of American exceptionalism. At the height of the crisis, with more than two thousand dying each day, Americans found themselves members of a failed state, ruled by a dysfunctional and incompetent government largely responsible for death rates that added a tragic coda to America's claim to supremacy in the world.

For the first time, the international community felt compelled to send disaster relief to Washington. For more than two centuries, reported the *Irish Times*, "the United States has stirred a very wide range of feelings in the rest of the world: love and hatred, fear and hope, envy and contempt, awe and anger. But there is one emotion that has never been directed towards the U.S. until now: pity." As American doctors and nurses eagerly awaited emergency airlifts of basic supplies from China, the hinge of history opened to the Asian century.

No empire long endures, even if few anticipate their demise. Every kingdom is born to die. The fifteenth century belonged to the Portuguese, the sixteenth to Spain, the seventeenth to the Dutch. France dominated the eighteenth, and Britain, the nineteenth. Bled white and left bankrupt by the

Great War, the British maintained a pretense of domination as late as 1935, when the empire reached its greatest geographical extent. By then, of course, the torch had long passed into the hands of America.

In 1940, with Europe already ablaze, the United States had a smaller army than either Portugal or Bulgaria. Within four years, eighteen million men and women would serve in uniform, with millions more working double shifts in mines and factories that made America, as President Roosevelt promised, the arsenal of democracy.

When the Japanese within six weeks of Pearl Harbor took control of 90 percent of the world's rubber supply, the U.S. dropped the speed limit to 35 miles per hour to protect tires and then, in three years, invented from scratch a synthetic rubber industry that allowed Allied armies to roll over the Nazis. At its peak, Henry Ford's Willow Run Plant produced a B-24 Liberator every hour, around the clock. Shipyards in Long Beach and Sausalito spat out Liberty ships at a rate of two a day for four years; the record was a ship built in four days, fifteen hours, and twenty-nine minutes. A single American factory, Chrysler's Detroit Arsenal, built more tanks than the whole of the Third Reich.

In the wake of the war, with Europe and Japan in ashes, the United States, with but 6 percent of the world's population, accounted for half of the global economy, including the production of 93 percent of all automobiles. Such economic dominance birthed a vibrant middle class, a trade union movement that allowed a single breadwinner with limited education to own a home and a car, support a family, and send his kids to good schools. It was not by any means a perfect world, but affluence allowed for a truce between capital and labor, a reciprocity of opportunity in a time of rapid growth and declining income inequality, marked by high tax rates for the wealthy, who were by no means the only beneficiaries of a golden age of American capitalism.

But freedom and affluence came with a price. The United States, virtually a demilitarized nation on the eve of the Second World War, never stood down in the wake of victory. To this day, American troops are deployed in 150 countries. Since the 1970s, China has not once gone to war; the U.S. has not spent one day at peace. President Jimmy Carter recently noted that in its 242-year history, America has enjoyed only sixteen years of peace, making it, as he wrote, "the most warlike nation in the history of the world." Since 2001, the U.S. has spent over $6 trillion on military operations and war, money that might have been invested in infrastructure at home. China, meanwhile, built its nation, pouring more cement every three years than America did in the entire twentieth century.

As America policed the world, the violence came home. On D-Day, June 6, 1944, the Allied death toll was 4,414; in 2019, domestic gun violence had killed that many American men and women by the end of April. By June of that year, guns in the hands of ordinary Americans had caused more casualties than the Allies suffered in Normandy in the first month of a campaign that consumed the military strength of five nations.

More than any other country, the United States in the postwar era lionized the individual at the expense of community and family. It was the sociological equivalent of splitting the atom. What was gained in mobility and personal freedom came at the expense of common purpose. In wide swaths of

America, the family as an institution lost its grounding. By the 1960s, 40 percent of marriages were ending in divorce. Only 6 percent of American homes had grandparents living beneath the same roof as grandchildren; elders were abandoned to retirement homes.

With slogans like "24/7" celebrating complete dedication to the workplace, men and women today exhaust themselves in jobs that only reinforce their isolation from their families. By the time a youth reaches eighteen, they will have spent fully two years watching television or staring at a laptop screen, contributing to an obesity epidemic that the Joint Chiefs have called a national security crisis.

Only half of Americans report having meaningful, face-to-face social interactions on a daily basis. The nation consumes two-thirds of the world's production of antidepressant drugs. The collapse of the working-class family has been responsible in part for an opioid crisis that has displaced car accidents as the leading cause of death for Americans under fifty.

At the root of this transformation and decline lies an ever-widening chasm between Americans who have and those who have little or nothing. Economic disparities exist in all nations, creating a tension that can be as disruptive as the inequities are unjust. In any number of settings, however, the negative forces tearing apart a society are mitigated or even muted if there are other elements that reinforce social solidarity—religious faith, the strength and comfort of family, the pride of tradition, fidelity to the land, a spirit of place.

But when all the old certainties are shown to be lies, when the promise of a good life for a working family is shattered as factories close and corporate leaders, growing wealthier by the day, ship jobs abroad, the social contract is irrevocably broken. For two generations, America has celebrated globalization with iconic intensity, when, as any working man or woman can see, it's nothing more than capital on the prowl in search of ever cheaper sources of labor.

For many years, those on the conservative right in the United States have invoked a nostalgia for the 1950s and an America that never was but has to be presumed to have existed to rationalize their sense of loss and abandonment, their fear of change, their bitter resentments and lingering contempt for the social movements of the 1960s. In truth, at least in economic terms, the country of the 1950s resembled Denmark as much as the America of today. Marginal tax rates for the wealthy were 90 percent. The salaries of CEOs were, on average, just twenty times that of their mid-management employees.

Today, the base pay of those at the top is commonly four hundred times that of their salaried staff, and many earn orders of magnitude more in stock options and perks. The elite 1 percent of Americans control $30 trillion of assets, while the bottom half have more debt than assets. The three richest Americans have more money than the poorest 160 million of their countrymen. Fully a fifth of American households have zero or negative net worth, a figure that rises to 37 percent for Black families. The median wealth of Black households is a tenth that of whites. The majority of Americans are two paychecks removed from bankruptcy. Though living in a nation that celebrates itself as the wealthiest in history, most Americans live on a high wire, with no safety net to brace a fall.

During the COVID crisis, 40 million Americans lost their jobs, and 3.3 million businesses shut down, including 41 percent of all Black-owned enterprises. Black Americans, who significantly outnumber whites in federal prisons despite being but 13 percent of the population, are suffering shockingly high rates of morbidity and mortality, dying at nearly three times the rate of white Americans. The cardinal rule of American social policy—don't let any ethnic group get below the Blacks or allow anyone to suffer more indignities—rang true even in a pandemic, as if the virus was taking its cues from American history.

COVID-19 didn't lay America low; it simply revealed what had long been forsaken. As the crisis unfolded, with another American dying every minute of every day, a country that once turned out fighter planes by the hour could not manage to produce the paper masks or cotton swabs essential for tracking the disease. The nation that defeated smallpox and polio and led the world for generations in medical innovation and discovery was reduced to a laughingstock as a buffoon of a president advocated the use of household disinfectants as a treatment for a disease that intellectually he could not begin to understand.

As a number of countries moved expeditiously to contain the virus, the United States stumbled along in denial, as if willfully blind. With less than 4 percent of the global population, the U.S. soon accounted for more than a fifth of COVID deaths. The percentage of American victims of the disease who died was six times the global average. Achieving the world's highest rate of morbidity and mortality provoked not shame but only further lies, scapegoating, and boasts of miracle cures as dubious as the claims of a carnival barker, a grifter on the make.

As the United States responded to the crisis like a corrupt tin-pot dictatorship, the actual tin-pot dictators of the world took the opportunity to seize the high ground, relishing a rare sense of moral superiority, especially in the wake of the killing of George Floyd in Minneapolis. The autocratic leader of Chechnya, Ramzan Kadyrov, chastised America for "maliciously violating ordinary citizens' rights." North Korean newspapers objected to "police brutality" in America. Quoted in the Iranian press, Ayatollah Khamenei gloated, "America has begun the process of its own destruction."

Trump's performance and America's crisis deflected attention from China's own mishandling of the initial outbreak in Wuhan, not to mention its move to crush democracy in Hong Kong. When an American official raised the issue of human rights on Twitter, China's Foreign Ministry spokesperson, invoking the killing of George Floyd, responded with one short phrase, "I can't breathe."

These politically motivated remarks may be easy to dismiss. But Americans have not done themselves any favors. Their political process made possible the ascendancy to the highest office in the land a national disgrace, a demagogue as morally and ethically compromised as a person can be. As Nate White quipped when asked why the British disdain Donald Trump, "There have always been stupid people in the world, and plenty of nasty people too. But rarely has stupidity been so nasty, or nastiness so stupid."

The American president lives to cultivate resentments, demonize his opponents, validate hatred. His main tool of governance is the lie; as of July 9, 2020, the documented tally of his distortions and false statements numbered 20,055. If America's first president, George Washington, famously could not tell a lie, the current one can't recognize the truth. Inverting the words and sentiments of Abraham Lincoln, this dark troll of a man celebrates malice for all and charity for none.

Odious as he may be, Trump is less the cause of America's decline than a product of its descent. As they stare into the mirror and perceive only the myth of their exceptionalism, Americans remain almost bizarrely incapable of seeing what has actually become of their country. The republic that defined the free flow of information as the lifeblood of democracy today ranks forty-fifth among nations when it comes to press freedom. In a land that once welcomed the huddled masses of the world, more people today favor building a wall along the southern border than supporting health care and protection for the undocumented mothers and children arriving in desperation at its doors. In a complete abandonment of the collective good, U.S. laws define freedom as an individual's inalienable right to own a personal arsenal of weaponry, a natural entitlement that trumps even the safety of children; in the past decade alone, 346 American students and teachers have been shot on school grounds.

The American cult of the individual denies not just community but the very idea of society. No one owes anything to anyone. All must be prepared to fight for everything: education, shelter, food, medical care. What every prosperous and successful democracy deems to be fundamental rights—universal health care, equal access to quality public education, a social safety net for the elderly and infirm—America dismisses as socialist indulgences, as if so many signs of weakness.

How can the rest of the world expect America to lead on global threats—climate change, the extinction crisis, pandemics—when the country no longer has a sense of benign purpose or collective well-being, even within its own national community? Flag-wrapped patriotism is no substitute for compassion; anger and hostility, no match for love.

Those who flock to beaches, bars, and political rallies, putting their fellow citizens at risk, are not exercising freedom; they are displaying, as one commentator has noted, the weakness of a people who lack both the stoicism to endure the pandemic and the fortitude to defeat it. Leading their charge is Donald Trump, a bone spur warrior, a liar and a fraud, a grotesque caricature of a strong man, with the backbone of a bully.

Over the last months, a quip has circulated on the internet suggesting that to live in Canada today is like owning an apartment above a meth lab. Canada is no perfect place, but it has handled the COVID crisis well, notably in British Columbia, where I live. Vancouver is just three hours by road north of Seattle, where the U.S. outbreak began. Half of Vancouver's population is Asian, and typically dozens of flights arrive each day from China and East Asia. Logically, it should have been hit very hard, but the health care system has performed exceedingly well.

Throughout the crisis, testing rates across Canada have been consistently five times that of the U.S. On a per capita basis, Canada has suffered half the morbidity and mortality. For every person who has died in British Columbia, forty-four have perished in Massachusetts, a state with a comparable population that has reported more COVID cases than all of Canada. As of July 30th, even as rates of COVID infection and death soared across much of the United States, with 59,629 new cases reported on that day alone, hospitals in British Columbia registered a total of just five COVID patients.

When American friends ask for an explanation, I encourage them to reflect on the last time they bought groceries at their neighborhood Safeway. In the U.S., there is almost always a racial, economic, cultural, and educational chasm between the consumer and the checkout staff that is difficult if not impossible to bridge. In Canada, the experience is quite different. One interacts, if not as peers, certainly as members of a wider community.

The reason for this is very simple. The checkout person may not share your level of affluence, but they know that you know that they are getting a living wage because of the unions. And they know that you know that their kids and yours most probably go to the same neighborhood public school. Third, and most essential, they know that you know that if their children get sick, they will get exactly the same level of medical care not only of your children but of those of the prime minister. These three strands woven together become the fabric of Canadian social democracy.

Asked what he thought of Western civilization, Mahatma Gandhi famously replied, "I think that would be a good idea." Such a remark may seem harsh, but it accurately reflects the view of America today as seen from the perspective of any modern social democracy. Canada performed well during the COVID crisis because of our social contract, the bonds of community, the trust for each other and our institutions, our health care system in particular, with hospitals that cater to the medical needs of the collective, not the individual, and certainly not the private investor who views every hospital bed as if a rental property. The measure of wealth in a civilized nation is not the currency accumulated by the lucky few, but rather the strength and resonance of social relations and the bonds of reciprocity that connect all people in common purpose.

This has nothing to do with political ideology and every-thing to do with the quality of life. Finns live longer and are less likely to die in childhood or in giving birth than Americans. Danes earn roughly the same after-tax income as Americans, while working 20 percent less. They pay in taxes an extra nineteen cents for every dollar earned, but in return they get free health care, free education from pre-school through university, and the opportunity to prosper in a thriving free-market economy with dramatically lower levels of poverty, homelessness, crime, and inequality. The average worker is paid better, treated more respectfully, and rewarded with life insurance, pension plans, maternity leave, and six weeks of paid vacation a year. All of these benefits only inspire Danes to work harder, with fully 80 percent of adults aged sixteen to sixty-four engaged in the labor force, a figure far higher than that of the United States.

American politicians dismiss the Scandinavian model as creeping socialism, communism lite, something that would never work in the United States. In truth, social democra-cies are successful precisely because they foment dynamic capitalist economies that just happen to benefit every tier of society. That social democracy will never take hold in the United States may well be true, but if so, it is a stunning indictment and just what Oscar Wilde had in mind when he quipped that the United States was the only country to go from barbarism to decadence without passing through civilization.

Evidence of such terminal decadence is the choice that so many Americans made in 2016 to prioritize their per-sonal indignations, placing their own resentments above any concerns for the fate of the country and the world, as they rushed to elect a man whose only credential for the job was his willingness to give voice to their hatreds, validate their anger, and target their enemies, real or imagined. One shudders to think of what it will mean to the world if Americans in November, knowing all that they do, elect to keep such a man in political power. But even should Trump be resoundingly defeated, it's not at all clear that such a profoundly polarized nation will be able to find a way forward. For better or for worse, America has had its time.

The end of the American era and the passing of the torch to Asia is no occasion for celebration, no time to gloat. In a moment of international peril, when humanity might well have entered a dark age beyond all conceivable horrors, the industrial might of the United States, together with the blood of ordinary Russian soldiers, literally saved the world. American ideals, as celebrated by Madison and Monroe, Lincoln, Roosevelt, and Kennedy, at one time inspired and gave hope to millions.

If and when the Chinese are ascendant, with their concentration camps for the Uighurs, the ruthless reach of their military, their 200 million surveillance cameras watching every move and gesture of their people, we will surely long for the best years of the American century. For the moment, we have only the kleptocracy of Donald Trump. Between praising the Chinese for their treatment of the Uighurs, describing their internment and torture as "exactly the right thing to do," and dispensing medical advice concerning the therapeutic use of chemical disinfectants, Trump blithely remarked, "One day, it's like a miracle, it will disappear." He had in mind, of course, the coronavirus, but, as others have said, he might just as well have been referring to the American dream.

5

OF WAR AND
REMEMBRANCE

EVERYTHING YOU KNOW OF YOUR LIFE, every sense you have of being modern, every existential doubt, each burst of confusion, every neurotic affirmation or affliction was born of the mud and blood of Flanders.

The Great War was the fulcrum of modernity. Jazz, Joyce, Dali, Cocteau, Hitler, Mao, and Stalin were all offspring of the carnage. Darwin, Freud, and Einstein were men of the nineteenth century, but their deeply unorthodox ideas—that species are mutable, that you do not control the sanctity of your own thoughts, that an apple does not fall from the tree as simply as Newton described—came to fruition and achieved general acceptance in the wake of the conflict, as if sown in soil fertilized by the dead.

For a century, Europe had been at peace even as industry and technology generated wealth and military power beyond anything that had ever been known. European nations consumed the world until the boundaries of colonial ambitions met and slowly tightened around the neck of civilization. Then a single bullet fired into the breast of a prince in Sarajevo in the summer of 1914 shattered a universe, a realm of certainty, optimism, hope, and faith, and in doing so sparked the greatest cataclysm in the history of humanity.

For a desperate month, people of all nations held their breath as those in power, no more than a hundred men, decided their fate. Hope for peace was bitterly betrayed. Born of another century, incapable of understanding a world that in a generation had been transformed by science, Europe's leaders were outflanked by history. With their peacock vanities and wrathful pride, their misplaced fidelities and pious certainties, cursed by a fatal and antiquated sense of honor, they stumbled toward the final hour before plunging their civilization into an abyss from which it would never emerge. The Second World War was but the child of the First. Winston Churchill called it another Thirty Years' War. Never was there a war less necessary to fight than the First, he wrote, or more essential to win than the Second. But it was all, he recognized, a single spasm of destruction.

At the outbreak of the conflict, in August of 1914, a man had to stand at least five feet eight inches to enter the British Army. Within two months, boys of five foot three were eagerly recruited. In eight weeks, the British Expeditionary Force, four divisions that represented the entire home army of the British Empire, had been virtually annihilated. In the first month of the war, the French lost seventy thousand men, forty thousand alone over two terrible days in August. Every month, the British Army required ten thousand junior officers alone to replace the litany of the dead. Public schools graduated their senior classes not to Oxford or Cambridge but directly to the trenches. The chance that any British male aged thirteen to twenty-four would survive the war in 1914 was one in three.

For the men in the trenches, the world became a place of mud and sky, with only the zenith sun to remind the living that they had not already been buried and left for dead. The regular army of the British Empire required 2,500 shovels a year. In the mud of Flanders, ten million would be required. Twenty-five thousand British coal miners spent the war underground, ferreting beneath the German lines to lay charges that detonated with such explosive force as to be heard on Hampstead Heath in London.

The sepia images that inform memories of the war, the tens of thousands of photographs taken in what was the first industrial conflict to be thoroughly documented on film, remain haunting and powerfully evocative. But the visual medium fails to capture two of the most dominant features of life at the front: the sound and the smell, the soul-crushing noise of prolonged bombardments and the constant stench in the trenches, an unholy combination of sweat, fear, blood, cordite, excrement, vomit, and putrescence. Staged images of men advancing, rifles and bayonets at the ready, belie the horror of helplessness that men actually experienced in an attack. Bayonets accounted for but a third of 1 percent of casualties. Rifle fire and machine guns brought down 35 percent of the dead and wounded. Most who died did so clinging in terror to the mud wall of a trench as a rain of steel and fire fell from the sky.

The concentration of suffering was unprecedented, in part because the zone of military operations was so small. For much of the war, the British front was a mere 85 miles in length, and at no time did it exceed 125 miles. The entire British sector, in which millions of men lived, trained, and died, extended only fifty by sixty miles, roughly the size of the English county of Lincolnshire. To supply and defend roughly a hundred miles of war front, the British would dig more than six thousand miles of trenches and lay down six thousand miles of railroad. The Ypres Salient in Belgium—a section of the battlefield surrounded on three sides by German forces—measured four miles by twelve; in that cauldron of death, 1.7 million boys and men would fall.

Among them would be many of the Canadian troops who sailed for England in the first week of October 1914. A British declaration of war had implied the participation of the dominions, and Canada, Australia, New Zealand, and South Africa rallied to the colors. The lads of Newfoundland, then a separate colony, sailed from St. John's on October 4 on HMS *Florizel*, heading through the Narrows and south to a rendezvous in the darkness with a flotilla of thirty-one ships. They were escorted by the 26,000-ton battle cruiser *Princess Royal*, which was transporting the 1st Canadian Division, along with nearly seven thousand horses, to England. The Atlantic crossing took eleven days. Following disembarkation at Plymouth, the force was transported to a training camp at Salisbury Plain. There they remained through a long fall and wet winter, soaked by two feet of rain in four months, twice the normal precipitation, as they drilled and marched and practiced all the skills deemed essential in the military training manuals, few of which would serve any purpose in France.

The Newfoundland Regiment was dispatched to Gallipoli, and the Canadians went to France, arriving in time to plug the British line at the Second Battle of Ypres. They were there on April 22, 1915, when the Germans attacked using poison gas for the first time in the history of warfare. Geoffrey Winthrop Young, a volunteer in the base hospital, recalled the day:

The bombardment seemed heavier and more menacing... I walked uneasily through our wards and offices. A wounded soldier, in the half coma we knew later as shell shock, was being tended and was muttering continuously "White faces... the moonlight... white faces." ... I went out. I could see figures running back, the yellow pall of cloud was higher, and again dots of figures in khaki were hurrying forward across the fields out to the northeast of us... The wounded began to pour in... the first poison gas sufferers. This horror was too monstrous to believe at first... But when it came, far as we had travelled from our civilized world of a few months back, the savagery of it, of the sight of men choking to death with yellow froth, lying on the floor and out on the fields, made me rage with an anger which no later cruelty of man, not even the degradation of our kind by the hideous concentration camps in later Germany, ever quite rekindled; for then we still thought all men were human.

If the Germans had stooped to a new low, the reputation of the Canadians soared to new heights, for it was only their heroic defense that stopped the assault at Ypres and held the British line, even as Allied forces on all sides panicked and fled the field. This was the beginning of what can only be seen as the transformation of a nation due to the martial skills of its soldiers. As the Canadian Expeditionary Force grew into a corps of four divisions, with over 400,000 men serving overseas, it proved to be not just a formidable fighting force but arguably the most innovative and imaginative command in the Allied armies. The battle roll reads as a complete record of the Western Front. In 1915, Canadians fought at Neuve Chapelle in March and Ypres in April, endured the collapse at Aubers Ridge in May and in September the disaster at Loos, a battle known to the Germans as der Leichenfeld von Loos, the Corpse Field of Loos.

Then came the Somme in the summer of 1916. In 140 days, the British advanced the line just six miles, leaving the Allies four miles short of Bapaume, which the General Staff had anticipated capturing on the opening day of the campaign. The British had in place 1,537 batteries, each capable of firing a thousand rounds a day.

As a prelude to the attack, for seven days the British unleashed a bombardment that grew to a sustained hurricane of piercing screams that hovered day and night over the entire length of the front. An NCO of the 22nd Manchester Regiment who survived the battle later recalled:

> The sound was different, not only in magnitude but in quality, from anything known to me… It hung over us. It seemed as though the air were full of vast and agonized passion, bursting now with groans and sighs, now into shrill screaming and pitiful whimpering, shuddering beneath terrible blows, torn by unearthly whips, vibrating with the solemn pulses of enormous wings. And the supernatural tumult did not pass in this direction or in that. It did not begin, intensify, decline and end. It was poised in the air, a stationary panorama of sound, a condition of the atmosphere, not the creation of man.

At the front, the Allied troops stumbled as the ground shook through their boots. A Canadian private wrote that "one's whole body seemed to be in a mad macabre dance… I felt that if I lifted a finger I should touch a solid ceiling of sound, it now had the attribute of solidity." Thirty million shells were fired, 600,000 Germans were killed or wounded, and after four months, the battlefield—a few score square miles—was covered in layers upon layers of corpses, three and four deep, bodies bloated, bones sticking up randomly from the ground, faces black with bluebottle flies.

To lie helpless in a trench in the midst of such an assault was, as one soldier recalled, like being tied to a post and attacked by an enemy wielding a sledgehammer. The hammer swings back for the blow, whirls forward, till, "just missing your skull, it sends the splinters flying from the post once more. This is exactly what it feels like to be exposed to heavy shelling." The blood rises to the head; fever burns the body; nerves, stretched to their limit, break. Men lose control, whimper and moan, and their eyes sink deep into sockets that will never again know the light.

And then there was the constant smell of decaying flesh, what remained of men caught on the wire, drowned in mud, choked by the oily slime of gas, reduced to a spray of red mist, quartered limbs hanging from shattered branches of burnt trees, bodies swollen and blackened skulls gnawed by rats, corpses stuck in the sides of trenches that aged with each day into the colors of the dead. Assigned to dig a communication trench to Delville Wood in the wake of an afternoon attack that had left four thousand dead, the commander of a British detachment went mad, as he found himself digging not through the chalk soils of Picardy but through bodily remains of those who had fallen in earlier attacks, cadavers stacked six feet deep, all of which fell apart to the touch.

At the Somme, the Canadians fought for four months, but the boys of Newfoundland perished in an hour. The regiment had returned from Gallipoli on the eve of the battle.

Attached to the British 29th Division, charged with the task of assaulting an impregnable fortress at Beaumont-Hamel, the Newfoundland Regiment was ordered over the top at 9:15 a.m. on July 1, the opening day of the battle. Their right flank hung in the air, because the 1st Battalion of the Essex Regiment, the next unit in line, had been delayed reaching the starting point by the sheer volume of dead. The lads barely got out of their own trench, and when they did, they floundered and died at their own parapet, their ranks swept by German machine-gun fire. Those few who advanced slowed and faltered, burdened by their loads, leaning and bowing into the storm as if to limit exposure to the lead. The British artillery barrage, timed to the second, had long since moved ahead and away from the immediate battlefield. Men dropped dead at every yard, and still the regiment pressed on. A few miraculously reached the German line, only to be shot down in the mud or skewered on the wire, which was not cut. The last thought of many of these brave men, breathless with exhaustion, blood-whipped and deranged with fear, was the horrid realization that the German line was utterly unscathed. Nothing had been damaged at all. The preliminary bombardment had missed. In fury, they spun into the wire, tossing grenades, their screams baffled by the throaty gurgle men sound when hit in the brain.

Altogether, 810 men of the Newfoundland Regiment went over the top that morning. Just thirty-five emerged from the battle physically unscathed. Every officer was lost, including three who should not have been in the attack at all. Only the commander and his adjutant survived to hear the praise of the General Staff. "It was a magnificent display of trained and disciplined valour," a senior staff officer told the

Newfoundland prime minister, "and its assault only failed of success because dead men can advance no further."

In the wake of the Somme, the Canadian forces came together under a single command rather than acting as reinforcements for the Allied lines, and for the rest of the war, the corps fought under the leadership of a Canadian, General Arthur Currie. If the British were led by men whose minds ran on rails and who sacrificed their soldiers as if on a mission to reduce the national population, General Currie brought insight and invention to the battlefield, qualities that resulted in one of the great Allied victories of the war, at Arras, in the spring of 1917.

The low fields of Flanders were flat and water-soaked, with few features rising more than two hundred feet above sea level. The slightest hill took on strategic importance. Looming over the British line was one dominant escarpment, five miles in length and rising nearly five hundred feet above the battlefield. The Germans had seized the heights of Vimy Ridge in 1914 and repulsed every subsequent British and French attack. Thousands had perished, and with each passing month, the position became more formidable as the Germans reinforced the command and enhanced defensive fortifications.

On Easter Monday, April 9, the Canadian Corps, 170,000-strong and fighting together as a single force for the first time, went over the top. Without benefit of a sustained preliminary bombardment, with new tactics that favored surprise and initiative, they overwhelmed the German defenses and within a day had taken most of the heights. Within three days, Vimy Ridge was theirs. It was the singular triumph of the Battle of Arras. Casualties included 3,598 killed and 7,004 wounded, terrible losses but modest by the standards of the war, especially given the scale and significance of the victory.

The unprecedented conquest at Vimy Ridge secured the reputation of the Canadian Corps, but it also meant that for the rest of the war, the force would serve as the shock troops for the Allied cause. Not four months later, the corps was transferred to Ypres to take part in Passchendaele, a battle that would be remembered by the historian A. J. P. Taylor as "the blindest slaughter of a blind war."

The goal was yet another fantasy of the British high command, a plan to break out of the Ypres Salient and capture Antwerp and the channel ports of Belgium. For the British and Canadian soldiers, it was the worst battle of the war. The ground was flat, sodden, shattered by shellfire. On the first night of the assault, the last day in July, the rains began, and except for a brief respite in September, they did not cease until November. Three thousand Allied guns fired more than four million explosive shells, nearly five tons of high explosive for every yard of German trench. The result was a muddy quagmire, a sea of black waste and shell holes, carcasses of horses and men, clouds of yellow and brown mist, an unbearable stench of rot and gangrene and the sweet scent of violets, which was the smell of gas and thus also the odor of death. To slip, wounded, off a duckboard was to drown in the fathomless morass. Gunners worked thigh-deep in water. To advance over open ground, soldiers used the bodies of the dead as stepping stones. On the day after the final assault, a senior British staff officer, Lieutenant-General Sir Launcelot Kiggell, made his first ever visit to the front. Reaching as far as his car could advance, appalled by the conditions, he began to weep. "Good God," he said, "did we really send men to fight in that?" The man beside him, who had been in action, replied flatly, "It's much worse farther up."

After three months, during which time the British suffered some 400,000 casualties, the village of Passchendaele, the objective of the first morning, had yet to fall. Once again, as at the Somme, it was noted in official documents that the British Army lacked the clerk power to tabulate the dead. The German high command compared Passchendaele to Verdun, a battle where more than a million French and German soldiers had been killed or severely wounded. "The horror of Verdun," wrote German general Erich Ludendorff, "was surpassed. It was no longer life at all. It was mere unspeakable suffering. And through this world of mud the attackers dragged themselves, slowly but steadily, and in dense masses. Caught in the advance zone of our hail of fire they often collapsed, and the lonely man in the shell hole breathed again."

The Germans simply fell back to a second and third line of defense. British generals begged their commander, General Haig, to call off the attack, but he refused. The village of Passchendaele fell to the Canadians on November 6. When the onset of winter finally drowned out the guns, Haig asked Sidney Clive, his senior liaison to French headquarters, "Have we really lost half a million men?" He had, for an advance of five miles. The corpses of more than ninety thousand British and Canadian dead at Passchendaele were recovered too severely mutilated to be identified. Forty-two thousand disappeared without a trace.

By the spring of 1918, the greatest security challenge for the Allied command was concealing the location of the Canadian Corps, whose presence at any sector of the front implied to the Germans an imminent assault. During the German spring offensive of 1918, the Canadians reinforced the French and British up and down the line. Then, in August, the Canadian Corps spearheaded the Allied counteroffensive at Amiens, the battle that turned the tide on the Western Front. The Canadians overwhelmed the enemy trenches, inflicting a defeat that caused Ludendorff to call August 8 "the black day of the German army." It was the beginning of what became known as Canada's Hundred Days, a nonstop engagement as the Allied forces, with the Canadian Corps in the vanguard, pushed the Germans east until their final surrender. The carnage continued until the end. The British and Canadian forces lost 300,000 men in just the final three months of the war. The guns fired literally until the eleventh hour. One of the last Allied soldiers to die was a Canadian private, George Lawrence Price, killed two minutes before the armistice went into effect. When word of the armistice spread up and down the line on November 11, it was greeted with relief and jubilation leavened by numb exhaustion, like the slow fading of a long and violent hallucination. The Allies had been preparing for another two years of war; many simply thought it would go on forever.

THE OLD MEN who had talked their nations into a war they could not escape had no idea of what they had wrought. For the moment, it seemed a tremendous victory. Germany and its allies lay prostrate. Russia was convulsed in upheaval and revolution, and France was bled white and reeling from losses from which it might never recover as a nation. The British emerged from the conflict with the most powerful army in the world, its navy supreme, its empire enhanced by a surge of colonial acquisitions that would not end until 1935, when it would finally reach its greatest geographical extent. That the war had destroyed the prosperity of a century of progress was not immediately evident to the average civilian still marching to the rhythms of tradition. That it had birthed the nihilism and alienation of a new century was a thought impossible to anticipate.

The truth lay in the numbers. Nearly a million dead in Britain and the dominions alone, some 2.5 million wounded, 40,000 amputees, 60,000 without sight, 2.4 million on disability a decade after the end, including 65,000 men who never recovered from the "twilight memory of hell" that was shell shock. In France, fully 75 percent of all men and boys between the ages of eighteen and thirty were either killed or wounded in the war. An entire generation was sacrificed to the carnage.

The victory had, in fact, bankrupted Britain. Before the war, the total cost of running the British Empire was roughly £500,000 a day. The war cost £5 million a day. Taxes and death duties alone provoked such economic agonies that between 1918 and 1921, a quarter of all English land changed hands. Nothing like it had occurred in Britain since the Norman Conquest.

For a decade, the social impact of the war spread as a slow wave throughout the far reaches of the Empire. Cremation, virtually unknown in Britain, Canada, and Australia before the war, became the preferred form of disposing of the dead for tens of thousands who had endured the sight and scent of death in the shell holes of no-man's-land. Daily exposure to that horror made cremation seem a clean, pure, and highly desirable alternative to burial.

Plastic surgery was also born of the war and the need to repair the shell-scarred faces of young boys who would live their lives behind wooden masks, attending special holiday camps where they might feel the wind on their gargoyle features without shame or humiliation.

If a generation of men had been lost, a generation of women had been left with few prospects for marriage and families. Single women, often traveling with a female companion, became a familiar sight on British trains and certainly a cliché of travel literature and popular culture.

Many people spoke of the war through the metaphor of dance. "By the end of 1916," Lady Diana Cooper famously remarked, "every boy I had ever danced with was dead." Vera Brittain, who lost her brother, fiancé, and two best friends, said that by the end of the war, there was no one left to dance with. The poet Stephen Spender remarked that the British middle class continued to dance, unaware that the dance floor had fallen out from beneath them.

IN EARLY 1919, the British government formed a peace committee to determine how to properly commemorate the victory. Its initial meeting, chaired by the foreign secretary, Lord Curzon, proposed a four-day celebration to be held in August 1919. Deemed a waste of money by veterans and with thousands of soldiers still awaiting demobilization, the event was scaled back to a single parade, scheduled for July 19. Tens of thousands of citizens descended on London to watch fifteen thousand servicemen parade past a temporary wood and plaster monument erected in Whitehall, a cenotaph dedicated to the "Glorious Dead." Had the actual dead walked abreast down Whitehall, the parade would have lasted more than four days. Had each man who died in the war been granted a single page upon which to inscribe his life, it would have yielded a library of some twenty thousand volumes, each six hundred pages long.

The men who had fought in the trenches encountered peace on very different terms. For many, as Paul Fussell wrote in *The Great War and Modern Memory*, travel became a source of irrational happiness, a moving celebration of the sheer joy of being alive. For these men, England offered only a memory of lost youth, betrayal, and lies, the residue of "four years of repression, casualty lists and mass murder sanctioned by Bishops."

The poet and composer Ivor Gurney had been gassed and wounded, and he died in 1937 still believing that the battle raged and he was part of it. Before his descent into madness, he had a moment of clarity. Returning from the front, and before he was institutionalized, he set out from Gloucester on foot to find a ship, any ship, that might take him away. H. M. Tomlinson, who nearly froze to death at Ypres, and whose memory was haunted by shellfire splintering the marble earth of winter, escaped as soon as he could to bask in the Caribbean sun and write exquisite elegies of the tropics. Maurice Wilson, who earned the Military Cross at Passchendaele and later had his arm and chest ripped open by machine-gun fire, a wound that never healed, wandered the South Pacific for a decade before conceiving a wild scheme to climb Mount Everest by fasting and mystic levitation. He bought a Gipsy Moth, learned to fly, and managed to reach Darjeeling, where he sold his biplane and, accompanied by two Sherpa guides, began the walk that would lead to his solitary death on the ice of the mountain.

Those who did go home, veterans who had lost years of their lives and endured unspeakable hardships, returned to a nation that wanted to forget everything about the war. They, too, wanted to forget. The poet Robert Graves and his friend T. E. Lawrence (who would eventually become known around the world as Lawrence of Arabia) famously made a pact never to speak of it. What they wanted was quiet.

But for Graves, as for many, it was impossible to escape the memories. There was always the night, waking in a pool of sweat, visions of bayonets and blood. Graves had enlisted at nineteen in the Royal Welch Fusiliers at the outbreak of the war. On July 20, 1916, in a reserve trench awaiting an attack on High Wood at the Somme, his battalion was caught by German artillery fire that left a third of the men dead and Graves seriously wounded. A metal splinter split his finger to the bone. Another metal shard went through his thigh, near the groin. Yet a third piece of shrapnel pierced his chest, slicing a hole through his body, destroying his right lung.

Unconscious, he was carried to a dressing station and left among the dead. Notice of his death reached his mother four days later, on his twenty-first birthday. His name appeared in the "honour roll" of the *Times*. But Graves, in fact, had survived the first night, and when the burial detail came by on the morning of July 21, he was found to be breathing. In agony, he was carried to a casualty clearing station, where, because of the sheer numbers of wounded, he lay on a stretcher in the summer heat for five days before finally being evacuated to a hospital at Rouen and then by ship and train to London. Two days later, he arrived at Victoria Station—immortalized by photographer Francis James Mortimer as the "Gate of Goodbye"—where the living and the dying crossed paths and crowds gathered throughout the war to receive the wounded home from the front.

Such an experience left Graves mentally unprepared for peace. He remained, as he recalled in *Goodbye to All That*, nervously organized for war. Shells burst above his bed as he slept. Strangers in the street assumed the faces of friends lost at the front. He could not use a telephone. Train travel made him ill. To encounter more than two people in a day cost him his sleep. He could not walk in a field without reading the lay of the land as if on a raid. The sound of thunder made him shake. A sharp report of any kind—the backfiring of a car, the slamming of a door—flung him face-first to the ground. The smell of cut lumber recalled the blasted pines and the corpses suspended from broken snags. His marriage dissolved, and he left England for Majorca, never to return to live in his native land.

On the war, Robert Graves remained mute, as did so many of his generation, because language itself had failed them. Words did not exist to describe what they had endured. After the war, as John Masefield wrote, one needed a new term for mud, a new word for death. The artist Paul Nash wrote that sunsets and sunrises had become "mockeries to man," blasphemous moments, preludes to death. Only the wordless, said Virginia Woolf, "are the happy." And only those who had fought understood. "The man who really endured the War at its worst," wrote Siegfried Sassoon, "was everlastingly differentiated from everyone but his fellow soldiers."

A graduate of Marlborough College and the University of Cambridge, a published poet and son of the landed gentry, Sassoon lived until 1967, but he would never write of anything that occurred after 1920. His six volumes of autobiography are the stories of a life that ended with the war. He expressed his anguish in verse, for his was a generation that still celebrated poetry as a real and meaningful literary form. The British Empire's elation at the outbreak of the conflict and its final descent to despair is readily tracked in the three most famous poems of the war: "The Soldier" by Rupert Brooke, John McCrae's "In Flanders Fields," and Wilfred Owen's masterpiece, "Dulce et Decorum Est."

Described by W. B. Yeats as a golden-haired Apollo, the most handsome man in England, Rupert Brooke, like many of his peers, had rallied to the flag in the fall of 1914. "We have," he told a friend, "come into our heritage." He joined the navy and later witnessed the siege of Antwerp. Three months into the conflict, the glory was gone. "It's a bloody thing," he wrote on November 5. "Half the youth of Europe blown through pain to nothingness, in the incessant mechanical slaughter of these modern battles. I can only marvel at human endurance." Upon his return to England, Brooke wrote "The Soldier."

> If I should die, think only this of me:
> That there's some corner of a foreign field
> That is for ever England. There shall be
> In that rich earth a richer dust concealed;
> A dust whom England bore, shaped, made aware,
> Gave, once, her flowers to love, her ways to roam,
> A body of England's, breathing English air,
> Washed by the rivers, blest by suns of home.

The poem, along with four other of Brooke's sonnets, was published in 1914 *and Other Poems*, a slim volume that in five years would go through twenty-eight printings. Brooke did not live to see its success. On April 17, 1915, en route to Gallipoli from Egypt, his ship stopped off at the island of Skyros, where, feverish, he wandered for several hours through olive groves scented with thyme and sage. By Thursday morning, April 22, he was comatose, his temperature rising by late afternoon to 106. The following day, he was dead of sepsis, brought on by an infected mosquito bite. He was buried in a "corner of a foreign field" on Skyros.

John McCrae was an older man, forty-three at the beginning of the war, a Canadian surgeon who served near Ypres in the terrible spring of 1915. Unlike Brooke, McCrae saw the worst of the fighting. The stress on such medical officers was intense and unrelenting. They were encouraged by social convention, decency, and military orders to do all that was possible to maintain good cheer. At the same time, as surgeons, they had to deal with an endless flow of carnage, working throughout the night as the guns roared and the flares and star shells lit up the sky, silhouetting ghostly figures in khaki wrapped in bloody blankets, labels dangling from limp bodies carried into tents where the flicker of acetylene lamps cast barely enough light for the doctors to determine the nature of the wounds.

In May, following the death of young Canadian officer and friend Alexis Helmer, McCrae wrote the fifteen lines of the poem that more than any other would distill the anguish of 1915, when there still remained hope that the conflict ultimately would have some redemptive meaning. He chose as a symbol of remembrance a delicate flower, unaware of the cruel irony that poppies flourished in the fields of Flanders only because constant shelling and rivers of blood had transformed the chemistry of the soil. "In Flanders Fields" survived the war, but McCrae did not. He died of pneumonia and meningitis at Wimereux, France, on January 28, 1918.

Brooke's and McCrae's poems, with their invocations of duty and honor, sacrifice and redemption, served the needs of a British government increasingly concerned about unrest and discontent on the home front. As early as the end of August 1914, the chancellor of the exchequer, David Lloyd George, and the foreign secretary, Edward Grey, had established the secret War Propaganda Bureau, the goal of which was to promote British war aims, both at home and abroad. In 1917, it was taken over by the Department of Information. By then, as Lloyd George, who had become prime minister, acknowledged, the "terrible losses without appreciable results had spread a general sense of disillusionment and war weariness throughout the nation." In a remark to C. P. Scott of the *Manchester Guardian* in December 1917, the prime minister added, "If the people really knew, the war would be stopped tomorrow."

The task of the Department of Information was to ensure that they did not know. In this, the closest allies of the government were the newspapers. Anything might be written as long as it vilified the enemy and propped up morale. "So far as Britain is concerned," recalled John Buchan, head of the department, "the war could not have been fought for one month without its newspapers." The truth itself became a casualty. "While some patriots went to the battle front and died for their country," wrote A. R. Buchanan, "others stayed home and lied for it."

It was precisely this duplicity that led Siegfried Sassoon to come out against the war in the summer of 1917. Wounded by a sniper's bullet through the chest, and later shot accidentally in the head by one of his own men, Sassoon had received the Military Cross and the Distinguished Service Order, medals he would one day toss into the Mersey. He had been deemed a hero, which made it especially awkward when his powerful manifesto was published in the *Times*:

> I am making this statement as an act of willful defiance of military authority because I believe the war is being deliberately prolonged by those who have the power to end it. I am a soldier, convinced that I am acting on behalf of soldiers. I believe that this war, upon which I entered as a war of defence and liberation, has now become a war of aggression and conquest… On behalf of those who are suffering now, I make this protest against the deception that is being practiced on them; also I believe that I may help destroy the callous complacency with which the majority of those at home regard the continuance of agonies which they do not share, and which they have not sufficient imagination to realise.

For a serving officer to publish such a tract was tantamount to treason. To avoid the embarrassment of a military court-martial, the government agreed to a compromise suggested by Robert Graves. Sassoon would be declared mentally unfit and dispatched to Craiglockhart, a military hospital in Edinburgh that specialized in the treatment of officers suffering from neurasthenia, or shell shock. It was there that he met Wilfred Owen. Owen had joined the 2nd Manchesters in December 1916 and within a week was at the front "marooned on a frozen desert," lying beside the stiff bodies of friends dead from the cold. For twelve days, he did not sleep, wash, or remove his boots. Under constant gas and artillery attack, with shells bursting within yards of his position, burying comrades alive, Owen shattered. He endured another three months until, shaking and tremulous, his memory vacant, he was evacuated from the front.

At Craiglockhart, Owen showed some of his unpublished poetry to Sassoon, who encouraged him to write about the war as the soldier actually experienced it. Inspired, Owen composed six poems in a single week. Among them was "Dulce et Decorum Est," considered by many to be the greatest anti-war poem ever written. The title comes from Horace, a line that had been inscribed in public school minds for generations: "It is sweet and proper to die for one's country."

> Bent double, like old beggars under sacks,
> Knock-kneed, coughing like hags, we cursed through
>   sludge,
> Till on the haunting flares we turned our backs
> And towards our distant rest began to trudge.
> Men marched asleep. Many had lost their boots
> But limped on, blood-shod. All went lame; all blind;
> Drunk with fatigue; deaf even to the hoots
> Of tired, outstripped Five-Nines that dropped behind.
>
> Gas! GAS! Quick, boys!—An ecstasy of fumbling,
> Fitting the clumsy helmets just in time;
> But someone still was yelling out and stumbling,
> And flound'ring like a man in fire or lime ...
> Dim, through the misty panes and thick green light,
> As under a green sea, I saw him drowning.

In all my dreams, before my helpless sight,
He plunges at me, guttering, choking, drowning.

If in some smothering dreams you too could pace
Behind the wagon that we flung him in,
And watch the white eyes writhing in his face,
His hanging face, like a devil's sick of sin;
If you could hear, at every jolt, the blood
Come gargling from the froth-corrupted lungs,
Obscene as cancer, bitter as the cud
Of vile, incurable sores on innocent tongues,—
My friend, you would not tell with such high zest
To children ardent for some desperate glory,
The old Lie: *Dulce et decorum est*
Pro patria mori.

Wilfred Owen returned to the trenches and later would win the Military Cross by singlehandedly seizing a German machine gun and using it to kill more of the enemy than he wished to remember. He would die seven days before the end of the war, leading his men in an attack across the Sambre-Oise Canal. Word of his death would reach his parents at Shrewsbury on November 11, 1918, as the church bells in their village tolled the news of victory and the armistice.

WITH THE PEACE, two million parents in Britain and the dominions woke to the realization that their sons were dead, even as the first of some three million veterans returned to a land socially and politically dominated by those who had not served. "I simply could not speak to such people," recalled Captain Herbert Read, who lost a brother in the last month of the war and was himself awarded the Military Cross and the Distinguished Service Order for valor, "much less co-operate with them. It was not that I despised them. I even envied them. But between us was a dark screen of horror and violation; the knowledge of the reality of war. Across that screen I could not communicate. Nor could any of my friends who had the same experience. We could only stand on one side, like exiles in a strange country."

For those who survived, life was precious but evanescent. They were not cavalier, but death was no stranger. They had seen so much that death had no hold on them. In the wake of a war that had betrayed the hopes and dreams of a generation, life mattered less than the moments of being alive.

When we listen today to the voices of these men, be it in poetry, diaries, or letters, all part of the cathartic flood of literature that came forth a decade after the armistice, what we hear is the cadence and reserve of a very different kind of man from any we might know or encounter today. Though the madness of what they endured spawned modernity as we know it, they remained scions of another time, a prewar era so removed from that of our own as to be utterly inaccessible—emotionally, psychologically, and spiritually.

And yet, though the Great War ended more than a century ago, it retains a powerful hold on our imaginations, not just because of the agonies that the conflict inflicted on so many millions of innocent lives. In what Winston Churchill called the blood-stained century of violence, even greater horrors would unfold. What draws us is the character of the men who fought and the values they embodied, traits that we admire to this day, if only because they are so rarely encountered in a culture obsessed with self. These, after all, were men of discretion and decorum, a generation unprepared to litter the world with itself, unwilling to yield feelings to analysis, yet individuals so confident in their masculinity that they could speak of love between men without shame, collect butterflies in the dawn, paint watercolors in late morning, discuss Keats and Shelley over lunch, and still be prepared to attack the German lines at dusk. They were men the likes of which we will never know again. Their words and deeds will endure as a testament for the ages. And perhaps for us the most amazing thing of all is that these men were our grandfathers.

6

THE CROWNING
OF EVEREST

WHEN EDMUND HILLARY AND TENZING NORGAY reached the
summit of Mount Everest on May 29, 1953, they stood on
·the shoulders of giants, their own comrades who had done
so much to position the team for the final assault. They also
owed a debt to the expeditions that had come before them,
the Swiss in 1952, four failed British attempts in the 1930s,
even the quixotic and lunatic trials of Maurice Wilson, a
soldier shattered in the Great War who died on the flanks
of Everest in 1934, convinced that mystic levitation alone
would allow him to reach the top of the world. But above all,
as Hillary often acknowledged, they climbed in the shadow
of the legendary British explorations of the 1920s, when
George Mallory and a remarkable team of naturalists, climbers, soldiers, and surveyors had marched 350 miles across
Tibet, walking off the map just to reach the flanks of a mountain that no European had approached at close quarters.

That Everest was the world's highest mountain had been
known since 1856, when the mathematicians of the Survey
of India had peered across the Himalaya at a white shard of
a peak scoring the horizon beyond Darjeeling. With pen-
cil and paper and the wizardry of differential calculus, they

determined that this "singularly shy and retiring mountain" was, in fact, 29,002 feet tall. In their calculations, carried out from a distance of over 100 miles, they were off by less than 50 feet. They named the mountain after the head of the survey, George Everest, whose family name was actually pronounced *Eave-rest*. A miserable man, widely disliked in India, his legacy was to have a mountain named in his honor yet mispronounced for all time.

Dreams of climbing Everest date to 1893, when Charles Bruce, a subaltern of the 5th Gurkha Rifles, and Francis Younghusband, an explorer and political officer already famous for his traverse of the Gobi Desert, came together on the polo grounds at Chitral on the Afghan frontier and first resolved to scale the mountain. The Raj naturally had other priorities. For decades, even as the British had expanded by sea, the Russians had done so on land, 55 square miles a day throughout the nineteenth century, bringing the ambitions of the czars to the gates of India, provoking a clash of empires famously celebrated by Kipling in the novel *Kim*, and known to the British as the Great Game, to the Russians as the Tournament of Shadows.

In 1904, convinced that Russians were making trouble in Lhasa, the British launched a preemptive invasion, with the goal of forcing Tibetans to align their interests with the Raj. Led by Younghusband, the force shattered Lhasa's isolation, only to encounter disappointment, for not a Russian was to be found. Retreating to India, Younghusband, who had never lost interest in Everest, dispatched a small mounted party under the command of Cecil Rawling to map the upper reaches of the Brahmaputra River and scout the approaches to the mountain. Britain at the time was famously engaged in the race to reach the North and South Poles, a competition the nation would ultimately lose. Everest loomed over the frontier of the Raj as a third pole, and Younghusband saw its conquest as a matter of imperial pride and ambition.

There was one small problem. Access through Nepal was out of the question, for its borders were closed to all foreigners. A Tibetan approach required permission from the thirteenth Dalai Lama, whose armies had just been crushed by the British. This left the challenge in the hands of intrepid adventurers who probed the mountain on their own, men such as the physiologist Alexander Kellas, the first foreign climber to recognize the unique talents of the Sherpas, and photographer John Noel, who stained his skin with walnut juice and in disguise reached within days of the mountain in 1913 before being turned back by a Tibetan frontier patrol. Upon Noel's return to London, plans were set in motion for an illicit assault, a clandestine expedition to be led by Cecil Rawling.

But then came the Great War. In the last years of peace, Geoffrey Winthrop Young, mentor of Mallory, had regularly hosted the best of British climbers at a mountain retreat in Wales, documenting the gatherings in a photographic album, the Pen y Pass diary. Of the honed and beautiful faces, no fewer than twenty-three would die and eleven be so severely wounded that they, like Young himself who lost a leg on the Italian front, would have to overcome immense physical impediments merely to be able to walk. When peace finally came, and thoughts turned again to Everest, Tom Longstaff, an old Himalaya hand, sent a laconic note to Younghusband that read simply, "The supply of young climbers is not what it was before the war."

Never spoken about and never forgotten, the war would hover over the Everest expeditions that finally got under way in 1921. Of the twenty-six British climbers who, on three expeditions (1921–24), assaulted the mountain, twenty had seen the worst of the fighting. Six had been severely wounded, including Jack Hazard, who climbed to the top of the North Col in 1924 with open bleeding wounds from the Somme saturating the cloth of his climbing tunic. Two others had been nearly killed by disease. One, John Noel, was hospitalized twice with shell shock. Four, as surgeons at the front, dealt for the duration with the agonies of the dying. Two lost brothers, killed in action. All had endured the slaughter, the coughing of the guns, the bones and barbed wire, the white faces of the dead. Howard Somervell, Mallory's closest friend on the mountain, found himself on the first day of the Somme surrounded by six acres of stretchers bearing the crumpled remains of men. After Everest, he would never again live in England, choosing instead to remain in India as a medical missionary, dedicating his life to saving the living that he might sweep away all memories of the dead.

Like many who had been too old to experience the carnage, Younghusband assumed that with the peace, the world would simply continue as it had before the war. Within a month of the armistice, he set in motion new plans for the mountain. The problem of access to Tibet was solved by a clever diplomatic initiative: an arms deal negotiated by the political officer and diplomat Charles Bell with the Dalai Lama, who needed a modern army capable of resisting Chinese aggression. With permit in hand, a passport signed by the Dalai Lama himself, the British sailed for India in April of 1921. Their goal was not to climb the mountain but to explore and map its approaches, seeking the "chink in its armour," a route that might allow for a successful assault the following year.

When George Bernard Shaw saw a portrait of the 1921 Everest expedition—the men dressed in Norfolk jackets, knickerbockers, and puttees; the geologist, Alexander Heron, in a camel hair greatcoat; the leader, Charles Howard-Bury, in Donegal tweed with matching dark tie and waistcoat; Mallory wrapped in a woolen scarf—he famously quipped that the entire scene resembled a "Connemara picnic surprised by a snowstorm." In a group photograph taken in Darjeeling on the eve of their departure overland for Tibet, the men do indeed appear less than heroic.

But appearances are deceiving. In 1905, Sandy Wollaston, the expedition's naturalist and physician, had on a day's notice traveled three months to join a botanical survey in the Ruwenzori Mountains in Uganda. He returned home by walking the entire length of the Congo. Four years later, he joined Cecil Rawling in New Guinea, marching a small army of naturalists, soldiers, convicts, and Dayak headhunters into the forests, where most would perish. In a lunatic scene in his journal, he describes a final supper, just him and the one other survivor seated at a camp table as rising floodwaters reach the level of their knees. To wash their dishes, they merely dip their plates beneath their chairs and continue their conversation.

Expedition leader Charles Howard-Bury had explored much of Central Asia. Drawn always to the sacred, he once embarked on pilgrimage along the waters of the Ganges, anointing his body with scented oils to receive the teachings of Sanskrit scholars. In one holy city, his reputation was made when he shot and killed a man-eating tiger that had carried off and eaten twenty-one fakirs, or holy men. A brilliant writer, he was fluent in no fewer than twenty-seven Asian and European languages. In 1913, he spent six months exploring the Tian Shan, the Mountains of Heaven. In a local market, he bought a baby bear, which he named Agu. He nursed and protected the cub throughout his expedition, carrying it with him on his horse and eventually bringing it home to Ireland. Agu grew to seven feet and lived out its life in the arboretum at the family estate at Belvedere. Wrestling with a mature bear from the Tian Shan would be, for Howard-Bury, his favorite form of exercise.

Yet another extraordinary figure in 1921 was an unsung Canadian hero, Oliver Wheeler. Seconded to the expedition by the Survey of India, Wheeler was tasked with mapping the inner massif of the mountain. He would spend more time higher on the mountain, exposed to its wrath, than any of the other climbers. And it would be he, not George Mallory, who would find the doorway to the summit, the passage up the East Rongbuk Glacier to the base of the North Col, the route that climbers from the north follow to this day. Mallory, who disliked Canadians, warmed slowly to the intrepid surveyor, but when the time came to climb the North Col, the one man he added to his team was Oliver Wheeler.

As they crested the Col, reaching higher than any other person had ever climbed, a wind like nothing they had known before plunged them into a maelstrom as mad and disorienting as anything Wheeler had experienced in France in all the noise, chaos, and shell blast of battle. Scarcely able to stand, he focused on his breathing, drew his hands around his face, and, with a discipline long ago honed in terror, slowed down the world until a new rhythm could be found and air inhaled during the lulls between the blasts of the gale. That night, as they huddled in exhaustion in their tent, Mallory stayed awake for hours, rubbing Wheeler's feet with whale oil, saving the life of the Canadian surveyor he had once disdained.

With the mountain's secret unveiled, the subsequent expedition, of 1922, began with great promise. The new leader was Younghusband's old comrade from Chitral, Charles Bruce. Known as the mad mountain maniac, Bruce was a soldier's soldier, ferociously strong and as delicate in action as a bull. At Harrow, he was revered for having established a school record for being thrashed by the headmaster more often and in a shorter period of time than any other student in the school's history. As a young man, he was so strong that he could with his arm extended lift a grown man, seated in a chair, off the ground to ear level. To keep fit, he regularly ran up and down the flanks of the Khyber Pass, carrying his orderly on his back. At Gallipoli, Turkish machine-gun fire had nearly severed his legs. He was sent home to convalesce, with strict medical orders never to walk uphill or climb stairs. No physician said anything about not climbing Everest.

The big question in 1922 was whether it was sporting for climbers to use oxygen. Men back in London who had never climbed anything higher than their desks felt it was improper to use supplemental gas. Those more scientifically inclined, such as Howard Somervell and George Finch, both members of the 1922 team, believed that augmenting one's equipment with oxygen was no different than seeking the finest pair of boots.

There was, in fact, a growing divide between those who still considered climbing to be a sport of gentlemen and a new generation who played in an altogether different league. The former used the language of war to describe their efforts and intentions on a mountain; the latter had lived through a war that allowed them to walk with grace and commitment at the very edge of death. In his contribution to the official account of the 1922 effort, Finch argued that the "margin of safety must be narrowed down, if necessary to the vanishing point." A climber on Everest must drive himself beyond exhaustion, "even to destruction if need be."

Finch expressed what all later climbers would come to know: there are no second chances on Everest. In 1922, Mallory, Somervell, Henry Morshead, and Teddy Norton set out as four climbing without oxygen, leaving Finch with no experienced partner. They suffered terribly, and at one point only a heroic move by Mallory kept them from being swept off the mountain to their deaths. Undeterred, Finch recruited to his team the general's young cousin, Geoffrey Bruce, a transport officer who had never climbed a mountain. Wearing down parkas, invented by Finch specifically for Everest, they would reach with oxygen higher and far closer to the summit than anyone before them. Despite this triumph, the expedition ended in disappointment and tragedy when, on the final push, an avalanche on the North Col swept seven Tibetan porters to their death. "Only Sherpa and Bhotias killed," Somervell later wrote. "Why, oh why could not one of us, Britishers, have shared their fate? I would gladly at that moment have been lying there, dead in the snow. If only to give those fine chaps who had survived the feeling that we had shared their loss, as we had indeed shared the risk."

The expedition that returned to the mountain in 1924 did so with a heavy burden, the full expectations of an entire war-stained nation yearning for redemption. At thirty-seven, George Mallory was already a legend. Teddy Norton would be elevated to expedition leader. Joining the team were Noel Odell, a veteran climber, and Sandy Irvine, a young Oxford scholar ferociously strong but with limited mountaineering experience. Recruited by Odell, Irvine, a mechanical savant, was responsible for maintaining and repairing the oxygen apparatus, now acknowledged as being essential for success.

Plagued by snow conditions that suggested the early onset of the dreaded monsoon, the 1924 team struggled for a month merely to establish a camp on the North Col. Beaten back repeatedly by weather, the expedition came to a fateful climax on the morning of June 6, 1924, as Teddy Norton said farewell to Mallory and Irvine as they made a final desperate attempt for the summit.

Time was of the essence. Though the day was clear, in the southern skies great rolling banks of clouds revealed that the monsoon had reached Bengal and would soon sweep over the Himalaya and, as one of the climbers put it, "obliterate everything." Mallory remained characteristically optimistic. In a letter home, he wrote, "We are going to sail to the top this time and God with us, or stamp to the top with the wind in our teeth."

Norton was less sanguine. "There is no doubt," he confided to John Noel, the expedition's photographer, "Mallory knows he is leading a forlorn hope." Norton knew the cruel face of the mountain. From the North Col, the route to the summit follows the Northeast Shoulder, which rises dramatically in several thousand feet to fuse with the North Ridge and ultimately the Northeast Ridge leading to the peak. Just the day before, he and Howard Somervell had set out from an advanced camp on the North Ridge at 26,800 feet. Staying away from the skyline and the bitter winds that sweep the Northeast Ridge, they had made an ascending traverse to reach the great couloir that clefts the North Face and falls away from the base of the summit pyramid to the Rongbuk Glacier ten thousand feet below.

Somervell gave out at 28,000 feet. Norton pushed on, shaking with cold, shivering so drastically he thought he had succumbed to malaria. Climbing on black rock, he foolishly removed his goggles. By the time he reached the couloir, he was seeing double, and it was all he could do to remain standing. Forced to turn back at 28,126 feet, less than 900 feet below the summit, he was saved by Somervell, who led him across the ice-covered slabs. On the retreat to the North Col, Somervell himself suddenly collapsed, unable to breathe. He pounded his own chest, dislodged the obstruction, and coughed up the entire lining of his throat.

By morning, Norton had lost his sight, temporarily blinded by the sunlight. In excruciating pain, he contemplated Mallory's final plan of attack. Instead of traversing the face to the couloir, Mallory and Irvine would make for the Northeast Ridge, where only two obstacles barred the way to the summit pyramid: a distinctive tower of black rock dubbed the First Step, and farther along the Second Step, a hundred-foot bluff that would have to be scaled. Though concerned about Irvine's lack of experience, Norton did nothing to alter the composition of the team. Mallory was a man possessed. A climber of stunning grace and power, he had on Everest already come close to death on three occasions. Veteran of all three British expeditions, he knew Everest better than anyone else alive.

Two days later, on the morning of June 8, Mallory and Irvine set out from their high camp for the summit. The bright light of dawn gave way to soft shadows as luminous banks of clouds passed over the mountain. Noel Odell, climbing in support, last saw them alive at 12:50 p.m., faintly, from a rocky crag, two small objects moving up the ridge. As the mist rolled in, enveloping their memory in myth, he was the only witness. Mallory and Irvine would not be seen or heard from again.

On Monday, June 16, the expedition abandoned the mountain. "We were a sad little party," Norton later wrote; "from the first we accepted the loss of our comrades in that rational spirit which all our generation had learnt in the Great War, and there was never any tendency to a morbid harping on the irrevocable. But the tragedy was very near. As so constantly in the war, so here in our mimic campaign Death had taken his toll from the best."

The disappearance of Mallory and Irvine would haunt a nation and give rise to the greatest mystery in the history of mountaineering. Some maintain that they reached the summit before meeting their end. Others have argued that weakened by dehydration, they could never have surmounted the impediment of the Second Step, a sheer wall of rock with deathly exposures on both sides. Still others have suggested that if the snows that battered the mountain, forcing the expedition to fall back in retreat not once but three times, had accumulated on the Northeast Ridge, the Second Step may have been covered, allowing the climbers to walk up the incline of snow with the very speed that Odell so famously reported. Had this occurred, surely nothing could have held Mallory back. He would have walked on, even to his end, because for him, as for all of his generation, death was but "a frail barrier" that men crossed, "smiling and gallant, every day." What mattered was not death, but how one lived.

Returning to Britain, in the wake of the battle, the survivors regrouped, still fully committed to the conquest of the summit. As if in defiance of the tragedy, the Everest Committee proceeded just as it had in the wake of the two earlier expeditions. Within a week of the memorial service at St. Paul's, Odell spoke at Queen's Hall. Somervell, identified by Arthur Hinks and John Buchan as another rising star, was soon delivering as many as three lectures a day, first in London and later at venues throughout the country. The great hope was commercial success for John Noel's *The Epic of Everest: The Immortal Film Record of This Historic Expedition*, scheduled to debut at the New Scala Theatre in London on December 8. The film was indeed a triumph, touring Britain and Germany, crisscrossing North America seven times; in Canada and the United States, more than a million people would see it. Ironically, the film's very success doomed any hope for an immediate return to Everest.

The death of Mallory and Irvine had forced Noel to reconfigure the film from heroic triumph to sublime tragedy. As if to distract the audience from the expedition's ultimate failure, he set out to create a total theatrical experience. Hiring a noted set designer, he transformed the stage of the New Scala into a Tibetan courtyard, with painted backdrops of Himalayan peaks illuminated in the haunting half shimmer of dusk. As the picture began, the lights would fade, temple doors open, and the curtain rise to reveal the flickering drama of another world. For an added touch of authenticity, Noel arranged to bring from Gyantse seven Tibetan monks, along with full ritual regalia: cymbals, copper horns, hand bells and swords, trumpets made from thigh bones, and drums crafted from human skulls. The monks, according to Noel's plans, would tour with the film, performing before every screening an overture of religious music and dances, setting the mood, as he put it, with "large doses of local colour."

The arrival of the "seven lamas" from India prompted newspaper coverage not likely to please the Tibetan authorities. Among the headlines in the *Daily Sketch*: "High Dignitaries of Tibetan Church Reach London; Bishop to Dance on Stage; Music From Skulls." Aristocratic Lhasa did not take kindly to the film's scenes of local men and women delousing their children and eating the lice. That seven monks had traveled abroad without the permission of their abbot, only to perform rituals on stage like some carnival show, provoked outrage, especially among the conservative monastic factions then ascendant in the Tibetan capital. Noel promoted his film as if it had emerged from a quaint and timeless void. In truth, Lhasa in 1924 teetered on the brink of revolution, with the fate of the nation in the balance.

At the center of the diplomatic firestorm was F. M. Bailey, warrior, diplomat, and spy, who had succeeded Charles Bell as political officer in Sikkim in 1921. If Bell tolerated the Everest expeditions, Bailey dismissed them as pointless provocations that compromised the key British diplomatic initiative in Tibet: the modernization of the country as a foil to the aspirations of both China and Soviet Russia. The thirteenth Dalai Lama, personally committed to the path of modernity, was actively opposed by the monastic orders, which wanted no European presence in Lhasa and certainly no British expeditions marching across the southern frontier of the nation, disturbing the deities and corrupting the people. Tensions in the capital were high, and there was even talk of overthrowing the Dalai Lama, an outcome certain to be disastrous for British interests.

In June 1924, even as Norton and Mallory made their final plans for Everest, Bailey traveled to Lhasa, officially to promote trade but with the actual goal of fomenting an uprising against the traditional religious orders. The key players were Tsarong Shapé, commander in chief of the army, and Laden La, the Darjeeling police inspector whom Bailey had sent to Lhasa some months before with the task of recruiting a two-hundred-man cadre to serve as the core of the rebel force. In the summer of 1924, Bailey himself remained in Lhasa for four weeks, meeting repeatedly with both Tsarong Shapé and the Dalai Lama. It is not clear what transpired, but in the end there would be no revolt. When Bailey returned to Sikkim, Tsarong Shapé joined him in exile, soon to be followed by Laden La. The traditionalists retained power, and a pronounced chill came over diplomatic relations between Tibet and the Raj.

With the Dalai Lama and the liberal factions in the army already on the defensive, Noel's film could not have come at a worse time. The Maharaja of Sikkim found the scenes of Tibetans eating lice so insulting that he banned John Noel from his kingdom. The Dalai Lama considered the entire extravaganza an affront to the Buddhist religion and called for the immediate arrest of the seven Gyantse monks who had gone abroad. The prime minister of Tibet sent a formal note to Bailey, demanding their immediate return; he ended his reprimand with the words the Everest Committee hoped never to read: "For the future, we cannot give permission to go to Tibet."

There would be no return to Everest in 1925. Within a year, John Noel's company, Explorer Films, would be out of business. When in 1926 the Everest Committee again sought permission to mount an expedition, Bailey did not deem it necessary even to forward the request to the Tibetan authorities. What became known as the "Affair of the Dancing Lamas" had profound and lasting political consequences. Reinforcing the strength of the traditionalists, it undercut the reforms of the thirteenth Dalai Lama, policies that no doubt would have placed Tibet in a much stronger position to cope politically and militarily with the Chinese onslaught of 1949 and the subsequent invasion that led a decade later to the death of a free nation.

As for Everest, it would not be until 1933, nine years after the disappearance of Mallory and Irvine, that another British climbing party would reach the base of the North Col. Two of the old veterans went along as transport officers, Colin Crawford from 1922 and E. O. Shebbeare from 1924, but the climbers were of a new generation: Eric Shipton, Wyn Harris, Bill Wager, Frank Smythe, and Jack Longland, all too young to have known the war. Only the expedition leader, Hugh Ruttledge, might have served, had not a hunting accident kept him on administrative duty in India for the duration of the conflict.

On the mountain that year, three men went high, Harris and Wager and then Smythe climbing alone the following day. Avoiding Mallory's route along the crest of the Northeast Ridge, they all traversed to the couloir, each managing to ascend just high enough to equal but not surpass Norton's height record of 1924. Nothing so grand would be achieved by subsequent British efforts. The reconnaissance of 1935 barely reached the North Col. An early onset of the monsoon repulsed the 1936 expedition, much to the chagrin of John Morris, who went along to organize transport. In 1938, heavy snow limited all movement; no one climbed higher than 27,300 feet. That Noel Odell at the age of forty-eight struggled to within a day of the summit was remarkable, but hardly enough to inspire a nation grown tired of the entire endeavor.

Britain in 1938 was no longer a land of grand imperial gestures. After a decade of stunned silence, scores of novels, memoirs, books of poetry, letters, and diaries had flooded popular culture, redefining the narrative of the war, laying waste to any remaining illusions of glory. The war to end all wars had ended nothing, save certainty, confidence, and hope. The Great Depression brought such misery that even those who were financially secure questioned the legitimacy of costly mountaineering expeditions, increasingly viewed as sport, that invariably resulted in failure. If achieving the summit of Everest had at one point been a symbol of imperial redemption, the record of six unsuccessful attempts was a reminder of national impotence.

The Everest Committee met for the last time on June 14, 1939, ten weeks before Hitler's invasion of Poland. At the Royal Geographic Society, Arthur Hinks, who as secretary to the committee had dedicated twenty years of his life to the quest, resigned the same day. There was talk of returning to the mountain, and permission was formally sought to launch expeditions in 1940, 1941, and 1942. Hitler's war buried such dreams, and by the time it was over, the Chinese Maoists were poised to take over Tibet and shut down all access to Everest from the north. In 1950, succumbing to pressure from Britain and the United States, Nepal opened its borders. British and Swiss expeditions probed the mountain from the south, along the axis that Mallory and his climbing companion Guy Bullock had scoped in 1921 when they peered down from the heights of the West Rongbuk Glacier to the Khumbu Icefall and the Western Cwm.

In 1953, victory came at last. Arthur Hinks, who had done all in his power to limit the Everest expeditions to proper British gentlemen, did not live to see headlines made not by Englishmen but by a beekeeper from New Zealand, Edmund Hillary, a farmer from the ultimate frontier of Empire, and a bold Nepali Sherpa, Tenzing Norgay, a man not simply ready for history but a figure destined to invert history itself, transforming in a single athletic accomplishment the very definition of what it meant to rule and to be ruled.

When Hillary and Norgay first returned from their triumph to base camp, Hillary motioned to Wilfrid Noyce, one of the other British climbers, and said simply, "Wouldn't Mallory be pleased if he knew about this?" A telegram celebrating their success reached London on the eve of the coronation of Queen Elizabeth II. Lest it overshadow the royal pageantry, the announcement was held back from the press for several hours. Only two people outside a small inner circle were immediately told the news: the Queen Mother and Lieutenant-Colonel Charles Howard-Bury, whose leadership during the 1921 reconnaissance had set the stage for the ultimate success.

It is now more than a hundred years since Howard-Bury first saw Everest looming against a lapis sky as his pony clip-clopped past a prostrating pilgrim on the dusty road to Tingri, where the expedition established its first base on June 19, 1921, one month and 362 miles after leaving Darjeeling. The very notion of Everest has been transformed by a century of desire, triumph, disappointment, and death. Well over five thousand men and women have reached the summit. Some three hundred have died trying; their bodies litter the mountain. In May, when the weather clears, climbers trudge toward the heights in such numbers that their narrow traffic, illuminated by headlamps in the darkness, can readily be seen from the valley floor. Commercial guides return to the mountain every year. Clients with the means to pay have a choice of services, which range from $35,000 to as much as $120,000, with no guarantee of success. To meet the demand, Sherpas have been known to summit twice in a week. Since 1994, Kami Rita Sherpa, a Nepalese climber, has reached the top no fewer than twenty-four times.

To recall a time when reaching the summit of Everest was as inconceivable as landing on the surface of the moon, as indeed was the case in 1921, is to reflect with reverence on the character of those who rose to the challenge. Their willingness to risk all carried them aloft. To this day, their spirit fires the heart of every climber from every nation who sets out to reach the summit of the world. No mountaineer could ask for a finer legacy.

7

THE ART OF EXPLORING

THE TRUE AND ORIGINAL EXPLORERS, men and women who actually went where no humans had been, were those who first left Africa, setting in motion waves of discovery as they and their descendants settled the entire habitable world, a feat fully accomplished some fourteen thousand years ago.

Since then, terrestrial exploration has rarely been divorced from power and conquest. Searching for a passage to the Indies, the French explorer Jacques Cartier is said to have discovered the St. Lawrence River in 1534, though the valley was clearly settled at the time and the waters offshore crowded with the Basque fleet, fishermen with no interest whatsoever in flaunting the location of their discovery, a cod fishery that would feed Europe for three centuries.

History heralds Francisco de Orellana as the first to travel the length of the Amazon, a journey undertaken in 1541. It was documented by his companion and scribe, Gaspar de Carvajal, who wrote of fleets of canoes and riverbanks dense with settlements, home to just some of the ten million people then living in the basin.

In one of the stranger episodes of the Spanish conquest, expeditions led by Gonzalo Jiménez de Quesada, Sebastián de Belalcázar, and Nicolás Federmann, coming from the north, south, and east, all reached the savannah of Bogotá. At a hastily assembled parlay, the three explorers agreed to sail immediately for Spain so that their king, Charles V, might determine who among them was the official discoverer of a place, roughly the size of Belgium, that was the domain of more than a million Muisca.

The twentieth century brought more of the same. Hiram Bingham shot to international fame and a place in the U.S. Senate with his "discovery" of Machu Picchu, an Incan site well known at the time to local farmers, who told him where it was and how to get there.

In 1921, George Mallory and his climbing companions walked off the map to find Everest, a mountain no one had approached at close quarters, save for the countless Tibetans they encountered as they trudged 360 miles across the plateau. Their arrival at Rongbuk, at the base of the mountain, made little impression. The Lama, Dzatrul Rinpoche, declined to break his retreat to greet them. In his *namthar*, a meticulous record of the spiritual and social life of the monastery, the arrival of the subsequent expedition, in 1922, earns but a few lines, including "I felt great compassion for them to suffer so much for such meaningless work."

Climbing to heights where oxygen deprivation obliterates consciousness, courting death, and placing at risk a precious incarnation and all of its potential for spiritual transcendence was, from the Buddhist perspective, an act of pure folly.

In the 1870s, Arctic exploration took a fateful turn from the practical and nautical to the personal and ultimately worthless, as men from several nations set their sights on the North Pole, a point on the ice with no intrinsic significance save as an emblem of physical achievement and national will. In many ways, this was the beginning of what would become in the twenty-first century an entire industry of adventure.

Reaching the North Pole was less a journey of discovery than a quest for personal glory and fame. Men such as Frederick Cook and Robert Peary clung desperately to their claims, often demonstrably false, even as they branded their expeditions indelibly with themselves. With endorsements, sponsorships, book deals, and lecture tours in mind, Robert Peary did nothing to share the glory with his indispensable companion, Matthew Henson; the four Inuit men who accompanied them both to the pole remain little-known footnotes to the story.

In 1897, twelve years before reaching the pole, Robert Peary kidnapped an Inuit family, including a young boy named Minik, and brought them to New York as living specimens. Minik's father soon died and the boy was put into the care of a staff member of the American Museum of Natural History. It was there that he came upon the skeletons of his father and the others on display in a diorama.

Minik survived twelve miserable years in the U.S. In 1909, he begged Peary to take him home, but Peary refused. By the time Minik finally returned to the Arctic, he was destitute, broken in body and spirit, lost between worlds, incapable of speaking his language, unable even to support himself as a hunter.

Back in Greenland, Minik came into the care of the greatest Arctic explorer of all time—Knud Rasmussen. In character, heart, motivation, and vision, Rasmussen was everything that Peary was not. What he achieved in a life cut short—he would die at fifty-four, having eaten an Inuit delicacy tainted with salmonella—a man of Peary's ilk could neither appreciate nor understand. An enameled faith in the superiority of his own culture left Peary half-blind, even as he stumbled north to the pole.

Rasmussen, by contrast, the son of a Danish missionary and a mother of Inuit blood, moved effortlessly between social and cultural realms, slipping in and out of roles with ease, garnering respect and affection in all that he did and in every hunting camp and settlement he graced. Not to mention the literary salons and theaters of Copenhagen and Paris, where, at the height of his fame as a writer, his star shone so brightly that guards had to be posted at every door to keep his female admirers at bay. Such notoriety came only after a lifetime of exploration and achievement; Rasmussen neither sought attention nor made much of it. What mattered to him was the Arctic and the story of a people who had found a way to survive in such a land.

Raised among West Greenlanders, knowing their language from birth, running his own dogs by the age of nine, Rasmussen could and did live as a native. He thought nothing of slipping naked beneath caribou hides to share his body heat with an elder. Like the Inuit, he didn't fear the cold; he made use of it. A moist skin left overnight was a shovel by dawn.

From an outpost at Thule in remote northwest Greenland, Rasmussen and Peter Freuchen, his partner in exploration, launched seven research expeditions between 1912 and 1933, all epic in scale. Their most ambitious effort, the Fifth Thule Expedition, consumed four years as they traveled overland from northern Greenland to the western limits of Alaska and the Bering Sea, twenty thousand miles altogether, all by dog team and sled. Nothing like it had been done in North America since Lewis and Clark.

Rasmussen did not undertake such journeys with endurance records in mind. He had no interest in being the first to do anything; his ambitions had nothing to do with self. Rather, his holy grail was not an object or a place but a state of mind, a depth of understanding that would allow him to reveal to the world the wonder of Inuit life. Stretching across the circumpolar expanses was a common culture of the northern ice: people speaking dialects of the same language, sharing beliefs and myths, responding to the same adaptive imperatives. Only one who had crossed a continent could report, as Rasmussen did, that a youth in Greenland would recognize a tale told by a grandfather on the northern slope of Alaska, just as that elder would know the folklore of northwest Greenland.

Though a child of the Arctic, an adopted son of the Inuit, Rasmussen never abandoned his fidelity to Denmark or his obligations as a writer and scholar to record his observations. The research contributions of the Fifth Thule Expedition, published in 1946, fill no fewer than ten volumes, six thousand pages altogether, with separate monographs dedicated to natural history, archeology, linguistics, and ethnography, along with photographs of some twenty thousand artifacts. These reports remain to this day a definitive source, offering an invaluable portrait of the Inuit before sustained and corrosive contact in the 1950s transformed their lives.

With his wizardly gift for languages and well-honed ethnographic eye, Rasmussen never doubted that the true glory of the Arctic resided in the genius and vision of the Inuit. His life's mission was to know the world as they did, to understand the patterns of their lives, to enter their realms of magic and shamanic power. With knowledge as his goal, cultural understanding his quest, Rasmussen completely redefined the promise and potential of exploration not only in the Arctic but throughout all the far reaches of the inhabited world.

IF RASMUSSEN REPRESENTS a certain ideal, a scholar of undaunted courage who lived a life of commitment and authenticity, the other end of the spectrum is occupied by colorful characters like my old friend the late Sebastian Snow, a sometime journalist eulogized in the British press as "an eccentric explorer... the last of the gentleman adventurers." Sebastian comes to mind whenever I hear of someone rowing a skiff across the Atlantic, base-jumping from some impossible height, or dying on Everest while waiting in queue to attempt the Second Step.

Sebastian and I met in Medellín in 1974 as he reached the city, having walked the length of South America from Tierra del Fuego. His goal was Alaska. As a boy, Sebastian had broken his thigh playing rugby at Eton, and doctors said he'd never walk again. His life's mission was to prove them wrong.

At twenty-one, Sebastian followed the Amazon from source to mouth, a journey only made possible by those hired along the way, local guides who did the heavy lifting and generally kept him alive. His first book, My Amazon Adventure, includes a foreword by Lieutenant-General Edward "Teddy" Norton, Mallory's close companion and the leader of the 1924 Everest expedition. Recalling his own experience with porters in Tibet, Norton goes out of his way to downplay the role of Sebastian's native companions, a disclaimer that speaks to a core conceit. "Without the driving power of the European," Norton writes, "these feats are not within the scope of local talent."

This was certainly true, but it was hardly an issue of character or the triumph of British pluck. The locals simply had other priorities in their lives and, from their point of view, better ways of spending their days.

By the time we met, Sebastian was forty-five, exhausted and well-worn, having walked 8,700 miles in eleven months. My job was to lead him through the Darién Gap, a notorious stretch of rainforest and swamp that separates Colombia from Panama, the one roadless passage on his intercontinental itinerary. The role fell somewhere between companion and "local talent." I hardly qualified as a guide, for I knew little about where we were going, which didn't concern Sebastian in the slightest. He courted trouble, just as he cultivated eccentricity, if only as fodder for his books.

Sebastian's long walk had been sponsored by a British newspaper, and his only obligation was to write periodic dispatches for a column that appeared on an irregular basis. Just what he had to say in these reports was something of a mystery. In eleven months, he had never strayed from the tarmac of the Pan-American Highway. In Ecuador, he had been joined for a few days by his old friend, the great British climber Chris Bonington. After a day, Bonington took to the hills, walking cross-country to relieve the boredom.

Sebastian spoke no Spanish and made no effort to pick up the language. If you speak the Queen's English loud enough, he claimed, anyone will understand. He lived by this adage, which was amusing but didn't inspire confidence that he had learned anything meaningful during his mostly solitary year on the road.

The book that ultimately emerged from his adventure, *The Rucksack Man*, features a breezy introduction by the well-known travel writer Eric Newby, another of Sebastian's friends. Newby's contribution, a tongue-in-cheek send-up of Sebastian, is as substantive as any passage in the book.

Hemingway said that the most important credential for a writer is to have something to say that the world needs to hear. Sebastian was a good man, but he failed this test as a writer. He had followed a highway the length of a continent while learning almost nothing of the people or the lands through which he'd moved. After so much effort, the story of his final journey—for sadly it would be the last—is distilled in a series of self-deprecating anecdotes that function largely to keep the narrative focused on the traveler, not the place.

Disregarded in its day and now long forgotten, The Rucksack Man, to be fair, was not the product of literary ambitions. Sebastian's genre was the Englishman out of his element, a perfect frame for his misadventures, recounted in his inimitable way. At twenty, I'd never been a character in a book before, and Sebastian could not have been more generous. Though I struggled to recognize myself in the stalwart companion he described, I certainly saw a person I aspired to be.

With the publication of The Rucksack Man, my writing appeared in print for the first time, albeit as passages from a journal that Sebastian lifted and passed off as his own, which seemed at the time a fair exchange. He obtained some much-needed content, while I saw my words alongside his, entire paragraphs, a juxtaposition that left me confident that if this mad but endearing Englishman could write books, so, too, could I. Only books, I promised in a flush of pride and purpose, that would have something to say, informed by original research, not photocopying, written and not simply typed, a lesson learned from The Rucksack Man, perhaps to a fault.

For my recent book *Magdalena: River of Dreams*, I came to know the river, the Mississippi of Colombia, in all of its dimensions, in all months of the year, with every shift of the seasons, from the headwaters in the Macizo Colombiano to the sand and stones of the Caribbean shore. At no point, however, was I tempted to paddle the Magdalena from source to mouth or to travel its length in a single journey, hitching rides perhaps on a series of barges and riverboats. Admirable as such achievements might be, my goal was not to produce a study of self, an account of a personal journey; it was to write a biography of Colombia through the metaphor of the river that made possible the nation. When in doubt, an author should always get out of the way. Building a narrative around self is to travel writing what false heroics are to exploration.

In the fifth century BCE, the Greek historian Herodotus traveled the length of the known world. Upon his return to Greece, he recounted a story from the Persian court, a morning when the emperor, Darius, gathered representatives of two of his subject peoples, one a culture that cremated its dead and the other a people who reputedly ate their dead. Darius asked each whether they might consider emulating the death rituals of the other. Both expressed horror at the thought.

Herodotus concluded from this the obvious: every culture favors its own traditions and looks down upon those of any other. Five centuries before Christ, this astute observer discerned the trait that more than any other has haunted humanity since the dawn of awareness: cultural myopia, the idea that our way is the right way and everyone else is a failure to be us, even if they don't know it.

Herodotus observed but did not judge. This is what made him so remarkable, and so vilified. Plutarch accused him of sympathizing with barbarians and urged that his memory be banished from Athens. Herodotus might well have avoided Plutarch's wrath had he simply recounted what he ate for breakfast, the names of the horses that had carried his kit, or how long it had taken to swim a river previously unknown to the Greeks and thus newly discovered by him.

Happily, for history, Herodotus recorded instead what he learned, phenomena that had nothing to do with his personal experience, what he saw beyond the shadow of self, the beauty of the land, the strange creatures of the marshes, the poetry of the people. He traveled as a sage, eyes wide open to wonder. His explorations took him beyond the exotic into new realms of knowledge and belief, the spiritual home of the curious, the limitless horizons of the human imagination as brought into being by culture.

At the very dawn of Western civilization, Herodotus recognized the human legacy as the subject most worthy of his explorations. Two thousand years later, Knud Rasmussen acknowledged the Inuit as the avatars of the Arctic. In a well-trodden world, new generations of explorers could do far worse than emulate their examples.

8

MOTHER INDIA

IT IS OFTEN SAID that India is more a state of mind than a national state, a civilization that has endured for thousands of years as an empire of ideas rather than one of territorial boundaries. Time and again, it has yielded to the onslaught of invaders but has always won in the end, absorbing foreign impulses and through the sheer weight of its history prompting mutations that inevitably transform every novel influence into something indelibly Indian.

The country is a paradox of wisdom and folly, generosity and greed. It's a land that invented monasticism and yet passionately celebrates the sensual. Among the world's most ancient civilizations, India is one of the youngest nations. A sea of immense poverty, it supports a prosperous middle class larger than the entire population of the United States, and no nation produces more PhDs.

The motherland of Hindu and Buddhist, Sikh and Jain, India is home to ten thousand faces of the divine—Rama, Vishnu, Shiva, Krishna, and Ganesha. And yet, having shown the world the universal possibility of nonviolence, it remains a cauldron of unrelenting violence between religious creeds.

Thanks to India, we reckon from zero to ten and use a decimal system without which our modern age would hardly be possible. Indians were the first to spin and weave cotton, gamble with dice, and domesticate chickens, elephants, and mangoes. They taught us to believe in the coexistence of contradictions and, better yet, to stand on our heads for good health.

The soaring arc of the Himalaya crowns the nation, running west to east for 1,500 miles, with fifty peaks over five miles high. Out of the mountains tumble the great rivers, the Indus, Brahmaputra, and Ganges, the Mother Ganga, considered by Hindus to be the essence of the divine. Geography aligns destiny with spiritual desire. Landscape serves as a temple for the gods. Culture springs from the power of the sun.

Heat is to India what rain is to England, a physical presence dictating the moods and patterns of the day, inspiring the way people dress, move, dance, and pray. Seen from the heights of Darjeeling, the vast Gangetic Plain is dotted with hundreds of small villages, all shimmering in the sun. As summer air rises over the subcontinent, moist ocean winds flow over the land from the southwest, forming great waves of clouds that herald the annual monsoon, the great cleansing rains that wash away sadness and despair, bringing fertility to the fields and as much as thirty feet of precipitation to the hill towns of the Himalaya.

With fifteen official languages, fourteen major language groups, and more than sixteen hundred distinct dialects, the entire subcontinent is a cacophony of cadence and human sounds. The average Indian market is more wondrous and surprising than any museum. The humblest village pulsates with more vitality, color, and scent than any carnival. Every day India bears witness to millions of small dramas worthy of Shakespeare, all enacted free of charge on countless stages beneath the laughter and sorrow of all the heavens.

BUT WHAT, IN FACT, IS INDIA? The word is of Greek origin, referring to the lands beyond the River Sindhu, as the Indus was known to Alexander the Great and his men. His armies turned back because they couldn't go on; the lands before them went on without end, with kings and rulers as numerous as their gods. The Mughals invaded in 1526 and controlled much of the drainage of the Ganges through 1853, but even they could not conquer all the immensity of the subcontinent.

The British ruled for two centuries, and at least one school of thought maintains that before the Raj, India was a meaningless notion and that the modern concept of India as a nation-state was only brought into being through British systems of administration, transportation, language, and law that imposed a semblance of unity on an impossibly diverse land—culturally, linguistically, and spiritually. This colonial conviction, set before our eyes even today like so many episodes of *Downton Abbey*, proved especially convenient for the British in the early years of India's national struggle for independence.

"What does the name India really signify?" asked Sir John Strachey, lecturing at Cambridge University in 1888. "There is no such country, and this is the first and most essential fact about India that can be learned. India is a name, which we give to a great region... There is no general Indian term that corresponds to it... We have never destroyed in India a national government, no national sentiment has been wounded, no national pride has been humiliated; and this is not through any design or merit of our own, but because no Indian nationalities have existed."

The Raj, if not India, was indeed a British invention, an imagined place defined by the ever-changing and expanding boundaries of political and commercial interests, which in turn were woven into reality by the mathematicians and technicians of the Survey of India. Maps were the key to the very notion of British India. They codified in two dimensions the geographic features of a subcontinent, even as they created the rationale for occupation. India the imagined landscape became concrete and meaningful when reduced to a map sheet, an exercise that stripped the land of cultural memory and meaning, allowing and even encouraging colonial authorities to believe that the thin veneer of their presence represented something more than it did.

British rule in India was in many ways a feint, an imperial sleight of hand. A cadre of a mere 1,300 men of the Indian Civil Service—none of them Indian—governed fully a fifth of humanity. The Indian Army was strong and well trained, but it numbered only 200,000; only a third were British regiments, and these dispersed from Siam to Persia. In much of the subcontinent, British authority resided solely in a single district officer, who spent each day in the saddle, moving from village to village, maintaining rule across thousands of square miles, with populations sometimes measuring in the tens of thousands.

The entire British presence in India depended on the presumption of power, which in turn was reinforced daily by ten thousand acts of domination and will intended to inculcate in the Indian people a sense of their inherent inferiority. This was the essence of colonialism. Image counted for everything. Lord Curzon, a stickler for pomp and protocol, as viceroy famously had his uniforms specially made by a theatrical designer in the West End of London. "There has never been anything," Curzon declared, "so great in the world's history as the British Empire, so great an instrument for the good of humanity."

Many Indians would disagree. In 1700, the Indian subcontinent was a highly prosperous realm producing, by one historical estimate, 27 percent of global GDP. Two hundred years of British rule drained the land of its natural capital, leaving it deindustrialized, looted, and impoverished. Famines during the last years of the Raj took the lives of 35 million. In 1947, Britain, having resisted Indian independence for decades, suddenly walked away, as it would do from all of its colonies, even as a religious divide exacerbated by years of colonial policies exploded in murderous sectarian violence between Hindus and Muslims.

If the agonies of partition affirmed the worst fears of Englishmen just home from the Raj, what actually became of India in the wake of independence defied all expectations, silencing those whose dire predictions had almost gleefully anticipated the collapse of the young nation. As Britain struggled to escape its own despair and destitution in the wake of two global wars, India came of age, drawing on strengths that had sustained its people through all the years of British occupation, and indeed through all of its long history as a civilization.

In laying claim to India as their creation, the British revealed, among many things, how difficult it was for them to view the world through any lens other than their own. Ruthlessly devoted to their mission of moral superiority, taught to disdain Hinduism as idolatry and superstition, each among them the product of an intellectual tradition which maintained that only things that could be seen and measured could be real, they struggled to understand that

India exists and has always existed as a land bound together by spiritual resonance, linked by the bonds of religious belief and practice.

This was the India I set out to find on my first visit to Varanasi, the ancient city on the Ganges known to the British as Banaras. My inspiration was a brilliant scholar, Diana Eck, whom I first met in Jaipur, soon after she had returned with a dozen of her students from the Kumbha Mela, the world's largest mass pilgrimage, a sacred gathering that once every twelve years draws forty million sadhus and seekers to the floodplain between the Ganga and Yamuna Rivers. A professor of comparative religion and Indian studies at Harvard, Eck is the author of *India: A Sacred Geography* and *Banaras: City of Light*, books that illuminate with insight, grace, and empathy a land forged not by the power of kings but by the power of ritual desire, delineated not by maps but by the footsteps of pilgrims.

FOR YEARS I HESITATED to travel to India, fearful perhaps that I'd be swept into all of its mysteries and never find my way home. When finally I reached Delhi, and later Darjeeling and the hill stations of Shimla and Dehra Dun, the deserts of Rajasthan, the cities of Agra and Amritsar, and the tropical shores of Kerala in the south, I struggled to make sense of a spiritual realm of bewildering depth and truly phantasmagoric complexity.

Drawn to the egalitarian philosophy of the Sikhs, I spent many joyful days at the Harmandir Sahib in Amritsar, where people from all walks of life and from all religions come together to worship as one. In the great hall, the Guru ka Langar, where some 35,000 people are fed each day, everyone sits together on the floor, all dressed in white, regardless of caste, race, or creed, as a symbol of the unity of all people, a notion at the core of Sikh beliefs and doctrine. A religious creed that focuses on the character of the individual, as opposed to their place in a preordained social and spiritual order, had obvious appeal. Every night I joined the volunteers along the bridge to the inner sanctum of the temple as the holy book, the Guru Granth Sahib, was passed hand over hand along a human conveyer belt, allowing pilgrims and visitors alike to touch the words of the divine, if only for a precious moment.

Far more challenging, indeed baffling to me, were the ancient Vedic traditions that prompted the Sikh reformation some five hundred years ago, spiritual devotions that reach back to the dawn of time and the very emergence of the oldest civilization in the history of the world. Father Locke, a Jesuit priest living in Kathmandu, famously concluded after years of diligent effort and study that trying to understand Hinduism was like trying to shovel mist. Father Locke had been raised in the shadow of one god. In India, there are said to be 330 million deities, 330 million distinct faces of the divine, all the infinite expressions of the Supreme Lord.

At its core, as Diana Eck explains, Hinduism is a tradition of pilgrimage to sacred places, of bathing in sacred waters and honoring divine images. It is a tradition in which all of the senses are employed in the apprehension of the divine. Shrines are piled high with fresh flowers, pungent with the scent of incense, alive with the chanting of prayers and the ringing of bells. It is a religion, she writes, that has imagined God and imaged God in a thousand ways, that has discovered the presence of the divine everywhere and has managed to bring every aspect of human life into the religious arena.

Of all the senses, it is with the eyes that Hindus best perceive the divine. They do not say, "I am going to the temple to worship," but rather "I am going for *darshana*," which means *seeing*. The goal is to have the *darshana* of the Lord and to receive from him the consecrated food offerings, the blessings of the divine. The thousands of statues and icons are not physical idols, mere representatives of the gods; they are actual lenses through which the ultimate truth may be clearly seen. They are doorways to the divine.

Within the Hindu cosmology, with its devis and goddesses, there is the great triumphant triad of Brahma the Creator, Shiva the Destroyer, and Vishnu the Sustainer, who strides across the universe, laying claim to heaven and earth and all the atmosphere that lies between. There are Rama and Krishna, the divine avatars of Vishnu, who sleeps on the Endless Serpent; Parvati, consort of Shiva; and Ganesha, the elephant-headed deity who brings good fortune, removing obstacles for the devout.

The mythic deeds of the gods are recorded as history in texts that are among the most ancient scriptures known. Eternal truths revealed by the sages, passed down orally for generations before being written down in Sanskrit as the four Vedas, including the Rig Veda, quite possibly the world's oldest religious text, and later the Upanishads, the foundation of Hindu philosophy and spiritual thought, and, of course, the great Sanskrit epics, the *Ramayana* and *Mahabharata*, composed long before the birth of Christ.

In monotheistic religions such as Christianity and Islam, we can trace the origins of the faith to a particular individual favored by God. In Buddhism, we learn of a luminous being who distilled a spiritual path of enlightenment based on ancient and multitudinous religious antecedents. In

Hinduism, we are talking about those very antecedents. The origins of the religion are enveloped in the mists of antiquity and a distant time when human beings began to look beyond the realm of nature spirits, beyond animism, to conceive of gods as living divinities, the moral arbiters of existence.

We can readily discern, for example, in contemporary Hinduism elements of the primordial rituals of those who worshipped the yakshas, the spirit beings of ancient India, before the emergence of Vishnu and Shiva in the first millennium BCE. Tree trunks daubed with orange pigment, swathed in string, sprinkled with water. A shrine of but two bricks surmounted by a slab of rock. A figurine of Ganesha smeared with vermillion and flowers. These are all signs of pre-Hindu and pre-Buddhist India, ritual practices that date back over three thousand years, still being honored today.

The Vedic traditions, Eck suggests, probably originated in ritual sacrifice, with fire altars being symbols of the entire universe. Only with the rise of theism did gods take center stage. Vishnu, Krishna, Shiva, Devi, even the Buddha emerged as focal points of a new type of religiousness. The deities were no longer local spirits, and their worship took on a new form, bhakti, meaning devotion, honor, and love. These were not local spirits to be propitiated, perhaps out of fear; these were gods worthy of worship and devotion. It is not clear when this spiritual metamorphosis occurred, but over the ten centuries that separated the first Buddhist empire in the fourth century BCE through the Gupta Empire of the fourth to sixth century CE, theistic Hinduism fully emerged, as indeed did Mahayana Buddhism.

What may appear to be a confusing and impossible assembly of deities, with all of their flamboyant deeds and mythological bravado, is, in fact, a completely coherent cosmology known and codified in the subcontinent long before the Christian era. One sees this—again, as Eck notes—in a comparison of early European and Hindu maps of the world. On early European maps, the frontiers of the unknown are depicted as such, often populated by dragons and other mythical creatures. Hindu maps of the cosmos are quite the opposite; they display a systematic whole. Nothing is left out. Nothing is set apart. The whole universe is a vast ecological system in which the primary life process is one of bursting forth, pouring forth, growing, flourishing, dying, decaying, withdrawing into seed form, and coming to life again. Everything is alive and interrelated. Everything is a symbol revealing the continuity between the human and the earthly and the cosmic realms.

In this cosmic scheme, there is one ultimate goal: freedom from rebirth. Life is cherished precisely because it is only through birth and life in this world that one can escape samsara and cross over to attain the ultimate spiritual achievement, moksha—freedom from rebirth. Death is more than an integral part of life; it marks the beginning of new life or, better yet, eternal freedom from the agony of rebirth.

ACCORDING TO HINDU MYTHOLOGY, at the beginning of time all the gods and demons called a truce, suspending their primordial conflict in order to behold in wonder, and together, the churning of the Kshirasagar, the celestial ocean of treasures. Among the fourteen cosmic treasures was amrit, the nectar of immortality. Jayant, son of Indra, fled carrying with him a tumbler of the precious fluid. For twelve years, demons pursued the god-king even as twelve drops of amrit fell to the earth. Four of these touched the ground at the sites of the contemporary cities of Haridwar, Prayagraj, Ujjain, and Nashik.

Since the time of the mystic sage Shankaracharya, every four years during the ritual of the Kumbh Mela, millions of spiritual seekers from all over India have gathered at one of these points of sacred geography (as Diana Eck and her students did). As the planets align and auspicious signs are seen in the sky, the entire flow of the Ganga is metaphysically transformed into amrit, nectar that sweeps away sin, cleansing the spirit and soul of everyone who immerses their bodies in the holy river.

"A flowing river," writes Gopal Krishna Gokhale, "is a flowing temple. There can be no better symbol of divinity."

Gokhale no doubt had in mind the Ganges at Varanasi, which rises from the western bank as the river takes a broad crescent sweep to the north. Known to Hindu mystics as Kashi, City of Light, Varanasi was an established center of pilgrimage and devotion two thousand years before the British Raj laid out the streets of Mumbai, Kolkata, Chena, and New Delhi. Imagine being able to visit Jerusalem or Rome and witness religious rituals as celebrated in the time of Christ. That is Varanasi today.

Long flights of stone steps, or ghats, reach like roots to the river, bringing pilgrims and worshippers to the water to bathe, even as the smoke of the cremation grounds brightens with the light of day. Dawn is the sacred hour. Facing east across the river, gathered in their thousands, the people—locals and pilgrims, visitors and sadhus—greet the rising sun with a crescendo of drums and bells, prayers and salutations, just as the people of Varanasi have done every morning for at least 2,500 years. The worship of the sun as a symbol of the divine, in many forms and with many names, is as old as India and as fresh as the light and warmth of each new day.

The Ganga is the river of India, a corridor of culture and commerce rising in the distant Himalaya and flowing 1,500 miles to the Bay of Bengal. The wandering sadhu, however, perched on a bench by the river, tells a different story. In the mythic realm, according to the Vedic texts, the headwaters are found not in the high mountains, as geographers maintain, but in the heavens, at the very foot of Vishnu, where the sacred river flows across the sky, white as the Milky Way. The Mother Ganga originally came to earth at the behest of an ancient king desperately in need of her help. Mercifully, as she plummeted from the luminous heights, her waters fell through the hair of Shiva, cushioning the fall as she tumbled upon the Himalaya and down to the great Indian plain.

Thus, Shiva became the bearer of the Ganga, and every wave and ripple of the river moves through his hair to this day. The river is the liquid form of Shiva's Shakti, his active and creative energy, his feminine essence, the fundamental force of life itself. Thus in bathing each morning in the Ganga, the pilgrims immerse themselves in the fluid of the divine. As liquid Shakti, the Ganga becomes the incarnation of the gods and the vehicle for all of Shiva's merciful work of salvation and creation.

In Varanasi, this coming together of the fire of Shiva with the cooling waters of the Ganga, again the liquid form of Shakti, is recalled in scores of small shrines throughout the city: erect stones known as lingas, all worn smooth with water and worship across the ages. A linga is not a phallus, despite the protestations of generations of British missionaries. The word means *emblem, symbol,* or *mark.* The shaft is Shiva, and the base, or yoni, is Shakti, symbols of the Supreme Lord's two kinds of power—his procreative generative power as husband of Parvati and his retentive power as an aesthetic and yogi. He is husband and aesthetic, creator and destroyer.

The linga thus is the visible symbol of the invisible, the form of the formless, the sign of Shiva's unfathomable presence as the eternal and transcendent Supreme Lord. Every time a pilgrim pours water on the linga of Shiva, they recall that cosmic moment when the Ganga fell to earth through the hair of Shiva. Without the Ganga, Shiva would remain the scorching brilliant linga of fire; without Shiva, the torrential force of the heavenly Ganga's fall would have shattered the earth. With water from the river, pilgrims in solemn rituals cool the fiery incandescence of the radiance of the gods, the water of the river being the nectar of immortality, the giver of grace.

As the Ganga crosses from heaven to the earth, the river remains a place of crossing from earth to heaven. It is for this reason that people from all over India come to Varanasi to live out their final days. For the Hindu, it is the point of origin of creation, the first place created by Shiva and Shakti, the locus from which the entire cosmos expanded. At the same time, Kashi is the universe, or at least a microcosm of it. Everything on earth that is powerful and auspicious is there—all the sacred places and all the sacred waters. All the gods reside here, attracted by the brilliance of the City of Light. Shiva dwells in the very rocks and earth beneath the city.

The Supreme Lord is everywhere, but in Kashi he lives with special intensity, always ready to bestow the enlightening wisdom of liberation. It is a place where the membrane between this world and the transcendent reality of the divine is so thin as to be virtually transparent.

The city illuminates truth and reveals reality. It enables one to see what is already there. People call this light the Eternal Shiva, and where the light intersects the earth, it is known as Kashi. And yet, mysteriously, Kashi is not of this earth. While it is in the world and at the very center of the world, it is not attached to the earth. It sits high above on top of the trident of its lord and protector, Shiva. It is not subject to the relentless movement of the great cycles of time, the eras of universal creation and dissolution. It is the still center, which anchors the perpetual movement of time and space, without participating in the ever-turning world of samsara.

The river is the liquid essence of the scriptures, the gods, and the wisdom of the Hindu tradition, the essence of Shakti, the energy and power of the Supreme, flowing in the life of the world. The River Ganges is every drop a goddess.

EVERY NIGHT IN VARANASI, cremation pyres flare along the riverbank. On the shore, a sacred fire always burns, maintained by Doms, a community of "untouchables." As a body arrives, after a family procession through the streets of the city, it is given a final dip into the Ganges. It is then sprinkled with sandalwood and decked in garlands of flowers, honored as if a god.

The chief mourner, generally an eldest son, takes flaming twigs of holy kusha grass from the eternal fire to the pyre. He circumambulates the pyre counterclockwise—everything is backward during the rituals of mourning. As he circles the pyre, his sacred thread, which normally falls away from the left shoulder, hangs from the right. He lights the fires, making of the dead an offering to Agni, the fire god; the flames convey the offering to heaven.

After the corpse is completely burned, the chief mourner performs a rite of the skull, cracking it with a long bamboo stick, thus releasing the soul from entrapment in the body. Now there is only ash. The mourner takes a clay pot of river water and throws it back over his shoulder upon the dying embers. He walks away without looking back. The members of the funeral party do not grieve openly, for it is said that tears pain the dead.

The subsequent rites for the dead last eleven days and include daily offerings of rice, providing symbolic sustenance for the transitional being as it makes its journey to the heavens, the world of the ancestors on the far shore. Feasts are put on for the Brahmins, who take nourishment on behalf of the deceased. On the twelfth day, the deceased is believed to reach its destination.

At death, the light is very intense, and what separates this world from the realm of eternity is almost transparent. Death is a time of clear seeing, vision, and insight. One's thoughts must be of the divine. As the fateful moment approaches, family and loved ones come close, as they whisper into the ears of the dying the names of the gods.

Death is the final event in this life, but in a sense, it is the first event in the life beyond. For Hindus, as Diana Eck writes, death is not the opposite of life; it is the opposite of birth. The procession of life includes the procession of death.

The key to spiritual freedom and liberation is wisdom, the enlightening wisdom of deep self-knowledge, which comes to all who breathe their last breath in Kashi. Within the holy city, Yuma, the god of death, has no authority. In Varanasi, death can be known, embraced, transformed, and transcended.

Just to walk the streets of the city is to be a pilgrim. To breathe the air is to embark on a spiritual journey. Every moment is a yogic gesture, for the city itself sanctifies every act. In Kashi, Shiva himself becomes the guru and imparts the enlightening wisdom to the dying, the light of wisdom communicated directly from God through the human ear to the human heart, the nectar words of infinite life. Flooded with the light of wisdom, one's soul can make the final crossing, riding the ferry of moksha, fording the river to realms that lie beyond life and death.

To end life in Varanasi implies spiritual liberation, which accounts for all the stones in all the temples, worn smooth over the centuries by the feet of pilgrims. They come to die in a city radiant in the light of faith, open to the rising sun and the distant shores of immortality. Death in Varanasi is not feared but patiently awaited, like the visit of a long-anticipated guest. And when it comes, the righteous dead are content to leave their bodies behind in the pyres, their funeral shrouds and garlands still damp from a last dip in the Ganga, a final blessing, even as the flames consume their physical remains.

WITH DIANA ECK'S PORTRAIT of Varanasi in mind, let's return to this question of India's identity. Was it really just the administrative skills of the British and the Mughals before them that brought into being the nation-state? Railroads and seaports, city grids and postal delivery, telegraphs and telephones, modern weapons and marble palaces? The answer, of course, is no.

India was born of spiritual aspirations, informed by myth, bound by conviction, tempered by ethics, inspired by morality. Wherever one goes in India, one finds a living landscape

in which mountains, rivers, forests, and villages are elabo-
rately linked to the stories of gods and heroes. The land bears
the traces of the gods and the footprints of heroes. Every
place has its story, as Eck writes, and every story in the vast
repository of myth and legend has its place.

The landscape not only connects places to the lore of
gods but also connects places to one another through local,
regional, and transregional practices of pilgrimage. These
tracks of connection stretch from this world toward the horizon of the infinite, linking this world with the world beyond.
And all of these patterns of sanctification continue to link
millions upon millions of Indians to the imagined landscape
of their country.

As it turns out, Kashi is not *the* Holy City; it is one of
many in a polycentric landscape, a sacred geography as vast
as the entire subcontinent in which everything is linked by
the tracks of pilgrims. There is not one River Ganga; there
are seven, each of a heavenly origin. The famous goddesses
of Varanasi are linked to networks of hundreds of goddesses.
Kashi is the earthly manifestation of Shiva's luminous
emblem, the sacred linga of light, but so, too, are at least
eleven other places in India.

On any given day, there are tens of millions of pilgrims on
the move. Pilgrimage is the essence of travel and tourism in
the country. The modern Indian goes on pilgrimage for any
number of reasons: to fulfill a vow, for family well-being, for
financial success or recovery, perhaps to bring the ashes of a
loved one to a sacred river, for spiritual purification, to seek
the wisdom of sages, or to behold the radiance of a place, to
take in its *darshana*.

Whatever the motive, pilgrims in their millions leave
home to enter a liminal space, taking on the hardships of the

open road in a quest for some higher goal. What they seek ultimately are points of illumination, sacred destinations known in India as *tirthas*, fords or crossing places charged with power and purity where heaven and earth come closely together, sometimes to meet, allowing the pilgrim to cross over the river of samsara to reach the far shore of liberation.

India is a land of ten thousand *tirthas*. As pilgrims travel, the tracks of their journeys create a circuit of meaning and connection, and it is this sacred matrix that ultimately defines the state of mind that is India.

Kashi, like a crystal, gathers and refracts the light of all pilgrimage places. All *tirthas* are present in Kashi, but Kashi is present as well throughout the land. Just as the essence of the Vedas may be packed into a single mantra, the infinite complexity of the divine may be perceived in a single deity, and the whole of the universe may be depicted in a cosmic map. Kashi condenses all of India in a great sacred circle, a geographical mandala. The entire city is the embodiment of Shiva, the sacred zone is an enormous linga of light, and light is wisdom.

For two thousand years, as Diana Eck concludes, the landscape of India has been made three-dimensional by the power of myth, narrative, and pilgrimage. The theme of a living cosmos has been continually sounded and continually heard. The mental map of India envisioned in the narratives of the sages, enlivened by the eruptions of the divine, and imprinted in the soil with the footsteps of millions of pilgrims remains to this day the most compelling and powerful force in India. All of India is one vast mandala of the sacred.

9

A NEW WORD
FOR INDIGENOUS

THERE ARE WORDS THAT, through overuse, lose their power and authority, causing the eyes to glaze over. *Sustainability* is surely one. *Indigenous* may be another.

As both a construct and a category, the term *Indigenous* first gained wide acceptance in the 1970s, elevated by anthropologists no longer comfortable with the language of their discipline. Referring to living peoples and cultures as *Indigenous* was certainly a step up from *primitive* and *savage*, words that appeared without shame in the early ethnographic literature.

Those for whom the concept was conceived embraced it as an essential part of their identity. The designation is today universally accepted, having been codified by national and international bodies, most notably in the 2007 United Nations Declaration on the Rights of Indigenous Peoples, which recognizes as Indigenous those "having a historical continuity with pre-colonial societies that developed on their territories" and who consider themselves distinct from the "societies now prevailing on those territories."

Indigenous, by this definition, embraces the myriad of cultures that have a shared history of subjugation and subservience and whose traditional homelands are today encompassed by the web of boundaries that mark the arbitrary limits of nation-states forged for the most part from the wreckage of nineteenth-century colonialism.

With power in all these new nations invariably consolidated in the hands of political elites, backed by militaries serving at the behest of the state, there is every reason for ethnic groups under threat to rally around a shared identity. As both a legal designation and a political declaration, the term *Indigenous* emerged as an essential expression of solidarity, eminently worthy of support and respect.

Still, the word is problematic. For one, it implies that some of us are, and others are not, indigenous to the planet, which is both incorrect and the wrong message to send to our children. Nurturing a spirit of place, displaying fidelity to land and water, and embracing with conviction the obligations of stewardship ought surely to be aspirations, indeed imperatives, for all people and all human societies. As the poet Gary Snyder wrote, "We must all become Native Americans, whatever our ethnic background, if there's to be any hope for ecological and cultural vitality on our shared Turtle Island." Snyder did not have in mind cultural appropriation; he was talking about the urgent need to change the way that we as humans inhabit this planet.

There is another issue. The great majority of the world's seven thousand languages—some 6,500 or more—are spoken by those deemed by academic convention to be Indigenous. But to wrap the lion's share of the world's cultural diversity in a single category, slapping upon it one word as if a convenient label, suggests a uniformity to culture that ethnography vehemently denies.

Every culture is the product of its own history. The Nenets reindeer herders of Siberia, the Barasana living in the forests of the Colombian Amazon, and the Dogon dwelling in the cliffs of the Bandiagara escarpment in Mali have no more in common culturally than the French, Russians, and Chinese do. Associating the former as *Indigenous peoples* is as arbitrary and ultimately meaningless as subsuming the latter into a contrived category of *industrial peoples*.

That such a bucket approach to culture also serves to reinforce a tired colonial stereotype goes largely unnoticed, oddly enough, even among those most earnest in their efforts to decolonize our thinking. To suggest that only some cultures are Indigenous implies, as noted, that there is another cohort of humanity that is something else. The astonishing sweep of the human spirit made manifest in thousands of cultures and expressed in the seven thousand voices of humanity is thus reduced to a single dichotomy: Indigenous and non-Indigenous, a dualistic opposition that has no more foundation in culture and history than the odious and deeply flawed distinction drawn throughout the nineteenth century between the *primitive* and the *civilized*.

The cultures of the world are not anonymous, as if lost in a fog of indigeneity. Every culture is a unique and ever-changing constellation of ideas and intuitions, myths, memories, insights, and innovations, all coming together to inspire an original vision of life itself. Each is its own response to a fundamental question: What does it mean to be human and alive? To compress this vast cultural repertoire into a single rubric ultimately diminishes all, denying to each culture its distinction—what it alone has distilled from the human imagination and our shared genius as a species.

If not *Indigenous*, what language or terminology should we use? Why not expand our concept of nations? Or reference ethnicities by name, with the respect that is due: Penan, Tuareg, Samburu, just three of the many hundreds of extant cultures with legitimate claims of sovereignty based on language and myth, traditional law, and deep histories of occupancy. Their voices are not vestigial. To the contrary, these are dynamic living peoples, fighting not only for their cultural survival but also to take part in the ongoing global dialogue that may well determine the fate of life on Earth.

If a language is but a dialect equipped with an army, then surely a nation is but a designation secured through diplomatic wrangling and the exercise of power. Geographical extent is as irrelevant as population size. A nation is what we declare it to be. Why not reimagine our concept of the state for a new era of respect and pluralism, environmental justice and stewardship, reciprocity and responsibility?

Though embedded in the province of British Columbia, the unceded territory of the Tahltan First Nation (36,100 square miles) encompasses more of the Earth's surface than any one of some eighty-five countries permanently represented in the General Assembly of the United Nations, among them Israel, Austria, Panama, Switzerland, and Kuwait.

Inuit in Canada alone—just part of a cultural realm that spans the Arctic from Greenland to Alaska and beyond—number more than the national populations of nine countries of the United Nations.

The geographical integrity of Haida Gwaii as the political and spiritual homeland of the Haida has been defined and delimited for at least six thousand years. Among the United

Nations, there are ninety-seven that did not exist before 1960. At seventy, I am older than more than a hundred countries recognized as such by the global community.

Within British Columbia, a family driving north from Vancouver to Prince George, a distance of five hundred miles, passes through more distinct languages than would be encountered by a traveler moving overland from Moscow to Madrid.

In the face of such astonishing cultural diversity, the word *Indigenous*, general to the point of inutility, loses all meaning and purpose; a well-intentioned rhetorical convenience that serves only to extend and augment historical efforts to erase identity. Were I to be among those so keen to decolonialize the English language, this word would have to go.

10

THE DIVINE LEAF
OF IMMORTALITY

AS DARKNESS FELL, the shaman lit a torch dripping in resin, and a red glow illuminated the circle of low stools where the Barasana men had gathered, as they do every night. From the other end of the *maloca*, the community longhouse, came the rustle of women and children making ready to sleep. A young man played an instrument made from the head of a deer; another blew softly over a large shell, a sound intended to stir the spirits. To one side, a boy kindled a fire beneath a large clay griddle, upon which he placed the leaves we had harvested earlier in the day. He tossed the coca with a steady rhythm, chanting and singing. His brother swept clean the dirt floor before setting fire to a large pile of dried leaves from the yarumo tree; the flames flared well over his head, then quickly died back, leaving a mound of white ash. Tobacco was passed, a powerful snuff that caused my head to spin and beads of sweat to soak my fingertips.

When the coca was ready, the leaves lightly toasted and brittle, the brothers placed several handfuls into the mouth of a large wooden mortar and began to pound them with a long pestle, taking turns. It was hard, steady work, and sweat soon fell from their brows.

Once the coca had been reduced to a bright green powder, they poured the contents of the mortar into a large calabash and mixed in some ash, roughly a handful for every two handfuls of coca. The color turned a rich gray-green. The next step involved wrapping the powder in palm fiber, securing the bundle to a stick, and shaking the contents vigorously inside a covered vessel. As small clouds of green dust filled the air, one of the men asked if I had ever tried mambe. At the time, I was only familiar with the coca of the highlands, where the leaves are taken whole, with alkali added to the quid. My new friend cringed at the thought. "Qué bárbaro," he said. "How barbaric."

He handed me the calabash. I followed his instructions and placed a large spoonful of the powder gently on my tongue. Within seconds, I coughed and great puffs of green smoke blew out of my mouth and nostrils. The Barasana roared with laughter. Never talk, I was told; just wait and let the mambe come together. I tried again and soon could feel the coca trickling down my throat.

The flavor was smoky and delicious. Within a few minutes, the inside of my cheek was numb and a mild sensation of well-being had spread throughout my body. It was a subtle feeling that lasted long into the night, even as the men spoke of the primordial journey of the Ayawa, the Thunders, the four culture heroes who brought order and harmony to the world, along with the gifts of the Anaconda, the sacred plants: tobacco, yagé, and coca.

The next morning, we left for the forest early. Fortified by a huge wad of mambe, I moved effortlessly over rough terrain and, for the first time, felt truly oblivious to the tropical heat. The renowned botanical explorer Richard Evans

Schultes, my professor at Harvard, used coca every day during his twelve years in the Amazon, beginning in 1941. It was no wonder. I smiled to recall how, like a sommelier recommending a favorite vintage, he had urged me to seek out the mambe of the Tanimuka, a delicious recipe, he claimed, infused with aromatic resin of a rare forest tree. Schultes once pulled out a can of mambe at a society party in Bogotá. In measured tones, he explained to anyone who would listen that the preferred ash came from the large palmate leaves of *Cecropia sciadophylla*, not the decidedly inferior foliage of *Cecropia peltata*. He naturally had the good stuff.

ON OCTOBER 31, 2020, WPVI, an ABC affiliate in Philadelphia, led its *Action News* evening report with a sensational account of a rare drug bust at Philadelphia International Airport. U.S. Customs and Border Protection (CBP) officers had seized more than twelve pounds of what was described as green cocaine, along with a mysterious "brown tar-like substance," which had tested positive for nicotine. The powder had tested positive for cocaine. According to authorities, the green hue was a way of camouflaging the drug, which through a chemical process using gasoline, ammonia, and other chemicals could be turned white, the implication being that ounce for ounce, it was just your ordinary blow, tinged with another color. "This seizure," reported Casey Durst, head of CBP's Baltimore field office, "perfectly illustrates how Customs and Border Protection officers use keen instinct and professional scientific analysis to intercept dangerous drugs being smuggled into our communities." In Cincinnati, port director Richard Gillespie heralded those singularly responsible for having "kept this dangerous green powder out of our neighborhoods."

Beneath the righteous pose, however, was a farce worthy of Molière. The source of the nicotine reported in the bust I knew well. It was ambil, a native paste with very high concentrations of tobacco, an addictive and potentially lethal drug that, when smoked, is responsible for the death of 480,000 Americans each year. Tobacco being legal, this substance was of no concern to the customs agents. The green powder in question was mambe. As early as 1957, Schultes had reported its use as a mild stimulant and essential component of the nutritional regime of the peoples of the Northwest Amazon; daily consumption more than satisfied the recommended dietary allowance for calcium, iron, phosphorous, vitamin A, and riboflavin. Prepared from an Amazonian variety of coca with notably low concentrations of the alkaloid, less than 0.5 percent dry weight, mambe is food as much as stimulant, as innocuous as a cup of black tea or coffee and far better for the health.

The news reports from WPVI noted that the "green cocaine" had been sent to labs in Savannah and Newark for analysis. Not reported were the results of the assays: trivial amounts of cocaine equivalent to the concentrations of caffeine in a coffee bean. Had anyone tried to snort the powder, they would have simply plugged their nostrils most unpleasantly with a substance the consistency of talcum powder; mambe is always consumed orally. To suggest that smugglers might import mambe to extract cocaine, even assuming it could be done given the large quantities of ash in the preparation, makes about as much sense as suggesting that someone would import Dom Pérignon to secure by chemical processing pure extracts of ethyl alcohol.

Like champagne, mambe is a specialized item, made with care and expertise on a small scale, a labor-intensive process that yields a highly valued and unique natural product. Drug cartels that have successfully shipped cocaine by the ton into the United States for nearly fifty years are not about to waste their time with it.

What transpired at the airport in Philadelphia was a drug bust on a par with Eliot Ness mistaking a truckload of potatoes for vodka and seizing the entire works as a violation of the Volstead Act.

It's one thing to note with regret that after fifty years of a "War on Drugs," there are more people in more places using worse drugs in worse ways than ever before. It's quite another to acknowledge that having spent billions of dollars a year on this misguided crusade—$1 trillion altogether—our frontline defenders still do not know the difference between a pure alkaloid first extracted as a drug in 1859 and coca, a benign and highly nutritious plant, revered today by millions and long celebrated by the ancient civilizations of South America as the divine leaf of immortality.

NEW DRUGS HAVE A WAY of upsetting the social order. The French Revolution was caused, at least in part, by caffeine. For generations, it had been impossible to drink the water in any European city for fear of succumbing to disease, cholera and dysentery in particular. People slaked their thirst with alcohol—gin and rum, whiskey, wine, ale, and mead. The entire continent was mildly besotted, which was fine as long as the main economic activities remained farming and handcrafted manufacturing.

Then, over the course of several decades, three botanical treasures appeared, all central nervous system stimulants: tea from India and China, chocolate from Guatemala, and coffee from Abyssinia by way of Brazil and the tropical lands of the New World. All had to be prepared with boiled water, which killed the pathogens, rendering them safe to drink. As each was a highly valued commodity, especially in the early years of the trade, their sale was concentrated in shops that, in time, became centers of intellectual and political intrigue, attracting the likes of Voltaire and Rousseau, Isaac Newton and Christopher Wren.

Rather than hanging out in the local tavern with their brows in their beer, those who patronized these new establishments became wired on caffeine, and they couldn't shut up. The writings of Alexander Pope, Samuel Pepys, and Jonathan Swift are positively infused with the drug. The coffeehouses of London and Oxford became known as penny universities, a reference to the cost of admission and the presence of the finest minds of the era engaged in open discourse and debate. Those of Paris served as fountains of revolution as equally talkative men took note that Louis XIV's chateau at Versailles was a bit bigger than their digs. The call to arms that led to the storming of the Bastille originated at the Café de Foy, Voltaire's favorite coffeehouse. From there, the mob gathered and marched.

Not surprisingly, those in charge, royalty across Europe and beyond, tried their best to curtail the use of the drug. In 1633, having imposed the death penalty for coffee drinkers throughout the Ottoman Empire, Sultan Murad IV stalked the streets of Istanbul in disguise, ready to decapitate anyone caught with the brew. Charles II infiltrated the coffeehouses of London with spies; in 1675, he ordered them all to close. As late as 1777, Frederick the Great of Germany attempted to outlaw coffee that his people might return to beer, which yielded a more docile and manageable citizenry.

A dull and passive work force was, in fact, the last thing the emerging industrial economy needed. One could harvest a field after a few tumblers of beer but hardly operate an unforgiving machine tool. Along with steam and coal, coffee and tea—two stimulants that kept workers alert while providing rare moments of relief and satisfaction—fueled the industrial revolution. A cup of tea became the salve for any crisis, even as the coffee break was institutionalized in every corporate office, union hall, school, hospital, fire station, and church priory, a brief but inviolable suspension of work allowing employees to imbibe with predictable regularity another dose of the drug.

Coffee, initially employed exclusively as a medicine and only later serving as a spark of sedition, had by the nineteenth century been tamed and domesticated, in good measure because it allowed industrial production to soar. Its pharmacology, the raw potential for good or ill, had not changed. Rats fed large doses of caffeine become aggressive and violent; a caffeine-crazed rat may even attack itself, ripping apart its own flesh. The drug's undoubted potential for harm, however, did not result in its prohibition; caffeine was needed, and thus its chemical essence was culturally redefined.

As a consequence, there is today no black market with extortionate prices that would bankrupt coffee drinkers and drive the most desperate among them to lives of crime while delivering enormous profits to those in control of the dark trade. Instead, coffee is sold at prices that reflect a healthy and dynamic free market, generating both legitimate employment and significant tax revenues for countries and governments throughout the world. What's more, the ready availability of the natural product—coffee beans and tea leaves in scores of flavors and blends—has effectively precluded the emergence of a significant market for chemical extracts of caffeine, which is fortunate. It is an axiom of pharmacology that the purer the drug, the greater the potential for abuse.

THE FIRST DRUG distilled in pure form from a plant was morphine. Cocaine was the second, isolated in 1859 by Albert Niemann, a German chemist. The drug came into its own in 1884, when Carl Koller, a close friend of Sigmund Freud, recognized its anesthetic properties, leading to the first application of local anesthesia in surgery. To this day, cocaine remains our most powerful topical anesthetic, notably for nose, throat, and ear surgery, a perfect illustration of the adage that there are no good and bad drugs, only good and bad ways of using them.

The Corsican chemist Angelo Mariani came down on the good side in 1863 when he patented Vin Tonique Mariani, a combination of Bordeaux red wine, coca leaf extract, and a sprinkling of pure cocaine. Needless to say, it was a hit. Mariani was responsible for two U.S. presidents, four kings, two popes, three princes, one Russian tsar, a shah, and the Grand Rabbi of France turning on to coca and cocaine. Pope Leo XIII carried a flask of the wine on his hip. In the United States, an ailing Ulysses S. Grant managed to complete his memoirs with the aid of a teaspoon a day for the last five months of his life. In 1909, Louis Blériot sipped Vin Mariani as he made the first flight across the English Channel. Among those who provided Mariani with testimonials were Thomas Edison, H. G. Wells, Jules Verne, Auguste Rodin, Henrik Ibsen, Sarah Bernhardt, and Edward, prince of Wales.

As the most popular prescribed medicine in the world, Vin Mariani inspired a host of imitators. In 1885, John Pemberton, a pharmacist in Atlanta, registered the trademark for a preparation called French Wine of Coca: Ideal Nerve and Tonic Stimulant. A year later, he removed the wine and added kola, an African nut rich in caffeine, as well as citrus oils for flavoring. Two years after that, he replaced the water with soda water, because of its association with mineral springs and good health, and he began to market the product as an "intellectual beverage and temperance drink." In 1891, Pemberton sold his patent to Asa Griggs Candler, another pharmacist from Atlanta, and a year after that the Coca-Cola Company was launched. Sold as a treatment for headache, a "sovereign remedy" for hangovers, Coca-Cola soon found its way into every drugstore in the land. The soda fountain, a kind of poor man's health spa, became an institution, and all over the country men and women were strolling into their pharmacies and ordering their favorite drink by asking for "a shot in the arm."

Although Coca-Cola removed cocaine from its formula in 1903, to this day it relies on the source plant as a flavoring agent. The Stepan Company in Maywood, New Jersey, imports tons of leaves every year, removing the cocaine to sell on the legal pharmaceutical market and then shipping the residue containing the essential oils and flavonoids to Atlanta. The company doesn't advertise its position as the only legal importer of coca in the country, but the leaves are the reason that Coca-Cola can legitimately lay claim to be, as its advertising slogan has long professed, the real thing.

By the 1880s, cocaine was being marketed and sold in scores of products: sweets, cigarettes, ointments, sprays, throat gargles, over-the-counter injections, and cocktails.

Articles in leading medical journals recommended cocaine for the treatment of a host of afflictions, ranging from seasickness to stomach pain, hay fever, depression, and even that scourge of the nineteenth century, female masturbation, for which one physician recommended a "topical dose to the clitoris for prevention." The wave of popularity peaked in 1884, the year Sigmund Freud published his misguided paper *On Coca*, in which he celebrated cocaine as a panacea, recommending it in particular for alcoholism and opium addiction.

It soon became apparent, however, that the cure could be worse than the disease. By 1890, the medical literature contained more than four hundred cases of acute toxicity brought on by the drug, psychotic episodes in which patients experienced horrific tactile hallucinations, haunting illusions of insects crawling beneath their skin. The reversal of fortunes was immediate and dramatic. Within a few years, cocaine went from being promoted as the most beneficial stimulant known to humankind, the tonic of choice of presidents and popes, to being perceived as a modern curse.

As laws increasingly circumscribed its use and availability, cocaine was condemned as a narcotic, which it is not, and culturally marginalized as a symbol of decadence, employed only by artists and assorted degenerates, most of them conveniently Black. As both physicians and politicians came to consider cocaine and morphine equally dangerous, coca became associated with opium, and the public was led to believe that the ruinous effects of habitual opium use would inevitably befall those who regularly chewed coca leaves. Thus, a mild stimulant that had been used for at least five thousand years before Europeans discovered cocaine came to be viewed as an addictive drug.

But coca is not cocaine, and to equate the leaf with the raw alkaloid is as misguided as suggesting that the delicious flesh of a peach is equivalent to the hydrogen cyanide found in every peach pit. Yet for nearly a century, this has been precisely the legal and political position of nations and international organizations around the world.

THE U.S. GOVERNMENT, in particular, has long demonized the plant. In Peru, programs to eliminate coca, supported by the United States, began fifty years before a black-market trade in cocaine existed. The real issue was not the drug but the cultural identity and survival of those who traditionally revered the leaves. The call for eradication came from officials and physicians, Peruvian and American, whose concern for the well-being of the Andean peoples was matched in its intensity only by their ignorance of Andean life.

In the 1920s, as physicians from Lima looked up into the Andes, they saw only abject poverty, illiteracy, poor health and nutrition, and high rates of infant mortality. With the blindness of good intentions, they searched for a cause. Since political issues of land, economic disparity, and raw exploitation struck too close to home, forcing them to examine the structure of their own world, they settled on coca. Every possible ill, every source of embarrassment to their bourgeois sensibilities, was blamed on the plant.

Carlos A. Ricketts, who first presented a plan for eradicating coca in 1929, described coca users as feeble, mentally deficient, lazy, submissive, and depressed. Referring in 1936 to Peru's "legions of drug addicts," Carlos Enrique Paz Soldán, a doctor and university professor, raised the battle cry: "If we await with folded arms a divine miracle to free our indigenous population from the deteriorating action of coca, we shall be renouncing our position as men who love civilization."

In the 1940s, the push for eradication was led by Carlos Gutiérrez-Noriega, chief of pharmacology at the Institute of Hygiene in Lima. Considering coca "the greatest obstacle to the improvement of Indians' health and social condition," Gutiérrez-Noriega established his reputation with a series of dubious scientific studies, conducted exclusively in prisons and asylums, which concluded that coca users tended to be alienated, antisocial, inferior in intelligence and initiative, and prone to "acute and chronic mental alterations" and other reputed behavioral disorders, such as "absence of ambition." The ideological thrust of his science was blatant. In a report published in 1947 by the Peruvian Ministry of Public Education, he wrote, "The use of coca, illiteracy and a negative attitude towards the superior culture are all closely related."

It was largely as a result of Gutiérrez-Noriega's lobbying that the United Nations dispatched a team of experts in the fall of 1949 to look into the coca problem. Not surprisingly, their findings, published in 1950 as the *Report of the Commission of Enquiry on the Coca Leaf*, condemned the plant and recommended a fifteen-year phaseout of its cultivation. Such a conclusion was never in doubt. Eleven years later, both Peru and Bolivia signed the Single Convention on Narcotic Drugs, an international treaty that called for the complete abolition of coca chewing and the end of coca cultivation within twenty-five years.

Incredibly, in the midst of this hysterical effort to purge the nation of coca, none of the Peruvian public health officials did the obvious: analyze the leaves to find out exactly what they contained. It was, after all, a plant consumed every day by millions of their countrymen and -women. Had they done so, their rhetoric might have softened.

In 1973, the Botanical Museum at Harvard, under the direction of Professor Schultes, secured support from the U.S. Department of Agriculture (USDA) to conduct the first comprehensive and modern scientific study of the botany, ethnobotany, and nutritional value of all cultivated species and varieties of coca. At the time, despite growing concerns about the illicit use of cocaine, surprisingly little was known about the source plant. The botanical origin of the domesticated species, the chemistry of the leaf, the pharmacology of coca chewing, the geographical range of the cultivated species, and the relationship between the wild and cultivated species all remained mysteries. No concerted effort had been made to document the role of coca in the religion and culture of Andean and Amazonian peoples since W. Golden Mortimer's classic, *History of Coca*, published in 1901.

Leading the research effort was the botanical explorer Timothy Plowman, whose mandate from the U.S. government, made deliberately vague by Schultes, was to travel the length of the Andean cordillera and locate, among other things, the place of origin of the sacred plant. It was the dream academic assignment of the 1970s, and it was my good fortune to serve as Plowman's field assistant for two years. Also on the trail of coca at the time was another Schultes protégé, Andrew Weil, then in the midst of a multiyear odyssey studying altered states of consciousness around the world. A graduate of Harvard Medical School with a profound knowledge of medicinal botany, Weil was fascinated by the healing properties of coca and the plant's role in nutrition and well-being.

With coca purchased in a public market in Bolivia, Plowman and Weil, in collaboration with James Duke of the USDA, examined fifteen nutrients found in the leaves, comparing their concentrations with the levels of the same nutrients in fifty common Latin American foods; coca was higher than the average in calories, protein, carbohydrates, and several minerals. The study also revealed that coca leaves contain a host of vitamins, more calcium than any other cultivated plant—especially useful for Andean communities that traditionally lacked dairy products—and enzymes that enhance the body's ability to digest carbohydrates at high altitude, an ideal complement for a potato-based diet. To the disappointment and horror of some of our backers in the U.S. government, the results confirmed that coca, as consumed by Indigenous peoples, serves as a mild and benign stimulant that is beneficial to the health and highly nutritious, with no evidence of toxicity or addiction.

As a physician, Weil went on to report that coca facilitates well-being, eases digestion, and demonstrably relieves the symptoms of altitude sickness, or soroche. His studies indicated that coca can be helpful in the treatment of rheumatism, dysentery, stomach ulcers, and nausea, with the leaves having a positive influence on respiration and a capacity to cleanse the blood of toxic metabolites, notably uric acid. Daily use of the leaves clears the mind, elevates mood, and tones and strengthens the digestive tract, enhancing the assimilation of foods, even while promoting longevity. Citing a popular Andean legend, Weil concluded that coca was indeed a gift from the heavens, a sacred leaf intended only to better the lives of all people dwelling in all places on the Earth.

NONE OF THIS will come as a surprise to students of South American history. For the Inca, coca figured prominently in every aspect of ritual and daily life. Before a journey, priests tossed leaves into the air to propitiate the gods. Unable to cultivate the plant at the heights of Cusco, they replicated it in gold and silver, in sacred gardens enclosed by temple walls. At the Coricancha, the Temple of the Sun, sacrifices were made to the plant, and supplicants could approach the altars only if they had coca in their mouths. Soothsayers read the future in the venation of the leaves and in the flow of green saliva on fingers, skills of divination acquired only by those who had survived a lightning strike. At initiation young Inca noblemen competed in arduous foot races, while maidens offered coca and chicha, a fermented drink. At the end of the ordeal, each runner was presented with a *chuspa*, a woven bag filled with the finest leaves as a symbol of his new manhood.

Long caravans carrying as many as three thousand large baskets of leaves regularly moved between the lowland plantations and the valleys leading to Cusco. Without coca, armies could not be maintained or marched across the vast expanse of the empire. Coca allowed the imperial runners, or *chasquis*, to relay messages across four thousand miles in a week. When the *yaravecs* (court orators) were called on to recite the history of the Inca at ceremonial functions, they were aided only by a system of knotted strings, called *quipus*, and coca to stimulate the memory. In the fields, priests and farmers scattered leaves to bless the harvest. A suitor presented leaves to the family of the bride. Official travelers lay spent quids of leaves on rock cairns dedicated to Pachamama and placed at intervals along the paths of the empire. The sick and dying kept leaves at hand, for if coca was the last taste in a person's mouth before death, the path to paradise was assured.

Just as the Inca venerated the plant, so, too, did the other peoples of the Andes. Archeological evidence suggests that coca was used as early as 3000 BCE at Valdivia on the Santa Elena Peninsula in western Ecuador; on the coast of Peru, it was commonly grown by 2500 BCE. Lime pots and ceramic figurines depicting humans chewing coca have been found at virtually every major site from every era of pre-Columbian civilization on the coast: Nazca, Paracas, Moche, Chimú. The very word *coca* is derived not from Quechua but from Aymara, the language spoken by the descendants of the Tiwanaku, the empire that predated the Inca on the altiplano and in the basin of Titicaca by five hundred years. The root word is *khoka*, a simple term meaning bush or tree, implying that the source of the sacred leaves is the plant of all plants. An active trade was established in the Bolivian highlands as early as 400 CE, one thousand years before the dramatic expansion of the Inca.

The plant itself is a beautiful if delicate shrub, with small white flowers and fruits the size and color of rubies. The texture and shape of the leaves vary, for there are two cultivated species, each with two distinct varieties. *Erythroxylum coca* var. *coca* is the classic leaf of the southern Andes, grown in the upper reaches of the tropical valleys that fall away to the Amazon, the harvest making its way to the markets of Cusco and La Paz. The coca of Colombia, *Erythroxylum novogranatense* var. *novogranatense*, is distinct. Adapted to hot, seasonally dry habitats and highly resistant to drought, it produces small narrow leaves of a bright yellowish-green hue. Named in 1895 after the colonial name for the country, Nueva Granada, this was the coca of the thirteenth-century Muisca and Quimbaya goldsmiths, the stimulant of the unknown peoples who carved the monolithic statues of San Agustín, the plant that Amerigo Vespucci encountered on the Paria Peninsula in 1499, when he recorded the first European description of coca chewing. Once extensively grown along the Caribbean coast of South America, in adjacent parts of Central America, and in the interior of Colombia, it is now found in traditional context only in the rugged mountains of Cauca and Huila and in the Sierra Nevada de Santa Marta.

Throughout Colombia, it is known as *hayo*. Curiously, the coca of the Northwest Amazon, *Erythroxylum coca* var. *ipadu*, the source of mambe, is derived not from hayo but rather from cuttings or seeds carried downriver from southern Peru or Bolivia in pre-Columbian times.

Finally, there is *Erythroxylum novogranatense* var. *truxillense*, now grown in the coastal desert valleys of northern Peru. With just a hint of wintergreen oil, this was the preferred coca of the Inca, not to mention the key ingredient in the secret formula of Coca-Cola.

Significantly, DNA analysis suggests that the progenitor of both domesticated species and all four varieties is *Erythroxylum gracilipes*, a wild species found the length of the Andes in the lowland forests of the western Amazon. Such botanical sleuthing may seem arcane, but to have two highly valued cultigens derived independently from a common ancestor, separate processes of artificial selection occurring thousands of miles apart, is an astonishing story of parallel invention, made all the more wondrous when the plants in question are revered throughout the entire range of the cultivated species as the very essence of the sacred.

IN THE WAKE OF THE CONQUEST, the Spaniards shattered every shrine, violated every temple, laid waste to an empire the scale and achievements of which they could not begin to fathom. All that was most precious to the Inca invoked the wrath of the conquerors, including coca, which was demonized as "the work of idolatry and sorcery," a plant serving only to strengthen "the wicked in their delusions, and asserted by every competent judge to possess no true virtues; but on the contrary, to cause the death of innumerable Indians, while it ruins the health of the few who survive."

That none of this was true ultimately proved convenient for the Spanish crown, especially as it became clear that the native people would not toil in the mines without access to the leaves. In 1573, with his eye on gold and silver, Francisco de Toledo, viceroy of Peru, revoked earlier laws prohibiting coca and, by decree, removed all obstacles to its cultivation. Even as he forcibly relocated much of the population to new settlements, condemning thousands to death—at Potosí alone, an average of seventy-five people would die each day for three hundred years—Toledo made sure the workers had coca.

Secularized and commercialized on a scale unknown to the Inca, coca became the foundation of the colonial economy, with taxes on its cultivation and exchange providing the church with its largest source of revenue. The Christian mission in Peru for three centuries was made possible by a plant the clergy had initially condemned as the "weed of the devil."

Many of the early chroniclers, scholars who sincerely sought to understand these newfound lands, wrote glowingly about the coca plant. In his *Royal Commentaries*, Garcilaso de la Vega stated that the magical leaf "satisfies the hungry, gives new strength to the weary and exhausted, and makes the unhappy forget their sorrows." Pedro Cieza de León, who traveled throughout the Americas between 1532 and 1550, noted: "When I asked some of these Indians why they carried these leaves in their mouths... they replied that it prevents them from feeling hungry, and gives them great vigor and strength. I believe that it has some such effect."

Throughout the colonial era and well into the nineteenth century, praise for coca was effusive, often taking a tone of reverence and devotion, even adulation. José Hipólito Unanue, the most famous Peruvian physician of the eighteenth century, heralded the leaves as a panacea, the most powerful herb in a healer's repertoire. The Swiss naturalist and explorer Johann Jakob von Tschudi, who spent five years in the Andes, was impressed by the longevity of those who, over the course of their lives, by his estimate, "have consumed no less than 2,700 pounds of leaves, yet nevertheless enjoy perfect health." Writing in 1846, he concluded, "I am clearly of the opinion that moderate use of coca is not merely innocuous, but even very conducive to health."

In Scotland, Sir Robert Christison, president of the Royal Society of Edinburgh (1868–73) and president of the British Medical Association (1875), decided to put the leaves to the test as he and ten students set out to walk thirty miles over hilly countryside, including an ascent of Ben Vorlich, which rises 3,232 feet above Loch Earn. "On arrival home before dinner," he reported, "I felt neither hunger nor thirst, after complete abstinence from food and drink of every kind for nine hours, but upon dinner appearing in half an hour, ample justice was done to it." At the time of his experiment, Christison was seventy-eight.

Such qualities, of course, had long been reported by scientifically minded travelers in South America. J. T. Lloyd, who published A *Treatise on Coca* in 1913, wrote of the native porters of Popayán in southern Colombia:

> After eating a simple breakfast, they would start with their heavy packs, weighing 75 to more than 100 pounds, strapped to their backs. All day long they traveled at a rapid gait over steep mountain spurs at an altitude that to us, without any load whatever, was most exhausting. On these trips the Indians neither rested anywhere nor ate at noon but sucked their wads of coca throughout the entire day. These Indians we found very pleasant, always cheerful, happy and good natured, in spite of the fact that their daily toil subjected them to the severest of hardships and the most frugal fare.

Lloyd concluded that coca was surely the key to their good health and good spirits. "Not only is it not harmful, it is said to provide nourishment for the body and to be useful in the treatment of many kinds of illnesses."

Perhaps the most fulsome praise came from the surgeon W. Golden Mortimer, author of *History of Coca* (1901). Among the more amusing testimonials is an account of the Toronto Lacrosse Club which, in 1877, while hosting the world championships, decided to use coca in all their matches. As Mortimer reported: "The Toronto Club was composed of men accustomed to sedentary work, while some of the opposing players were sturdy men accustomed to out of door exercise. The games were all very severely contested, and some were played in the hottest weather of one summer; on one occasion the thermometer registered 110F in the sun. The more stalwart appearing men were so far used up before the match was completed that they could hardly be encouraged to finish the concluding game, while the coca chewers were as elastic and apparently free from fatigue as at the commencement of play."

Mortimer acknowledged coca as a panacea, noting its virtues as a medicine, tonic, and food. But what truly fascinated him was the subtlety of its mode of action. It was a stimulant to be sure, and yet, at the same time, its subjective effect on the body was unlike that of any other stimulant known to science. As the physician W. S. Searle wrote in 1881, "It is not a little remarkable that while no other known substance can rival coca in its sustaining power, no other has so little apparent effect. To one pursuing the even tenor of his usual routine, the chewing of coca gives no especial sensation, in fact the only result seems to be a negative one, an absence of the customary desire for food and sleep. It is only when some unusual demand is made upon mind or body that its influence is felt... Those expecting some internal commotion or sensation are disappointed."

Andrew Weil captured this quality of the coca experience beautifully in his description of his first exposure to mambe while visiting the Cubeo in the Colombian Amazon in 1973. The effect of coca, he reported, was so subtle that it could not be compared to any other natural product similarly employed; it had to be learned to be appreciated, with set and setting playing a significant role.

His first taste of mambe occurred at night, leaving him with a good feeling "that lasted for some time after I had nothing more in my mouth; in fact, it never really ended but simply trailed off imperceptibly." It was only in the morning, as he huddled with the men as they exchanged a calabash full of the delicate green powder, that he came to understand what all the fuss was about. "I found myself marching along in the column of Cubeos, swinging my machete, humming a tune, and feeling increasingly happy. The coca seemed stronger at this hour of the morning. Its warm glow spread from my stomach throughout my body. I felt a subtle vibrational energy in my muscles. My step became light, and there was nothing I wanted to do more than just what I was doing."

THE DIFFERENCE between coca and cocaine, anthropologist Enrique Mayer once quipped, is the difference between traveling by donkey and traveling by jet plane. A clever line, but one that misses an essential point. The actions of coca and cocaine are not comparable. Each gives a sense of well-being, but while cocaine assaults the central nervous system, the effect of coca is modified by any number of naturally occurring compounds found in the leaves and not present in cocaine.

Indigenous people who have traditionally used and celebrated coca show no preference for leaves with high levels of the alkaloid. The preferred leaves are always those rich in aromatic compounds and essential oils and low in cocaine. Mambe is made from leaves that have the lowest concentrations of cocaine of any of the cultivated varieties.

What's more, the cultures of coca and cocaine consumption could not be more different. What draws people to cocaine is the exotic decadence, the mystique of a rich man's drug, the ritual of a handful of the select few slipping into the shadows of a party to snort a few grains of a mysterious crystal that these days could be just about anything. Inclusion in the clandestine circle in the corner of the room, the stall in the bathroom, a private office at work declares that one has arrived. Everyone at the party knows what is happening, which again is intentional. One of the privileges of membership in a secret society, as anthropologists have long reported, is the right to periodically flaunt the secrecy in public. Otherwise, what's the point of belonging? A lingering legacy of the cocaine culture of the 1980s is a small epidemic of hepatitis C, contracted by those who in their youth found it glamorous to stick up their noses a $100 note, damp with the snot of a stranger.

Coca, by contrast, is less a high than a meditation. Consumed in the Colombian Amazon as mambe, the plant is more commonly taken as whole leaves, which are held in the mouth as a quid for about forty minutes and then removed and placed on the ground in a respectful and deliberate gesture. To chew coca, or at least to efficiently absorb the small amount of the alkaloid in the leaves, one must modify human saliva by the addition of alkali. Any basic compound—baking soda, ash, limestone—will do. The Barasana and Makuna fire yarumo leaves to secure the ash. The Kogi and Arhuaco of the Sierra Nevada de Santa Marta, mountains that soar to twenty thousand feet above the Caribbean coastal plain of Colombia, prefer seashells, which they acquire by trade or gather as part of elaborate pilgrimages to the ocean.

For the Mamos, the sun priests of the Kogi and Arhuaco, the chewing of hayo is the most profound expression of culture. Their spiritual ideal would be to refrain from sex, eating, and sleeping while staying up all night, chewing the leaves, and chanting the names of the ancestors. As the guardians of the world, they believe that their rituals and prayers maintain the cosmic and ecological harmony of nature. At night, before they rest, they taste the leaves, deep in contemplation of the day that has passed; in the morning, hayo welcomes a new dawn. Every adult man consumes roughly a pound of leaves each day, beginning at marriage and continuing until his final breath.

In the mountains of the southern Andes, distance is measured not in miles but in *cocadas*, the length of time that a traveler is sustained by a single chew of leaves. When people meet on a trail, they pause and exchange k'intus of coca, three perfect leaves arranged to form a cross. They then turn to face the nearest of the Apus, the protective mountain deities that hover over every community and direct the destinies of all those born in their shadows. With eyes lifted toward the summits, they bring the leaves to their mouths and blow softly, a ritual invocation that sends the essence of the plant back to the earth, the community, the sacred places, and the souls of the ancestors.

The exchange of leaves is a social gesture, a way of acknowledging a human connection. But the blowing of the *phukuy*, as it is called, is an act of spiritual reciprocity, for in giving selflessly to the earth, the individual ensures that in time the energy of the coca will return full circle, as surely as rain falling on a field will inevitably be reborn as a cloud. This subtlety of gesture is, in its own way, a prayer for the well-being of the entire world.

The etiquette of *hallpay*, the totality of the act of using coca—the exchange and salutations, the way one places the leaves in the mouth, the attitude of reverence and respect—in a very real sense defines what it means to be Runakuna, a child of Pachamama. Throughout the entire Andean world, as anthropologist Catherine Allen writes, "One cannot function as a social being unless you partake in the ritual, and you must do it properly." Nothing causes more offense than tourists and travelers who stuff their mouths with leaves, like horses eating hay.

Whether the leaves are taken in the presence of a friend or a stranger, alone or together with all the community, to chew coca, to *hallpay*, is to transcend self and become part of the social, moral, and spiritual nexus that in the Andes gives meaning to life. Coca alone makes possible direct communication with the divine, with some saying today that the first to taste the leaves was Santísima María, mother of Christ, who according to legend lost her holy child and chewed on the leaves to allay her grief.

Thus, for the people of the Andes to be without coca is a form of social and spiritual death, an excommunication from existence itself. Efforts to deny the Runakuna access to the leaves, to eradicate the traditional fields, are not analogous to outlawing, for example, beer in Germany, coffee in the Middle East, or betel chewing in India. They are the policies of cultural genocide.

THE WAR ON DRUGS began in 1971, when Richard Nixon concocted the drug crisis strictly as a political ploy to galvanize his base ahead of his reelection campaign in 1972. At the time, most Americans had never heard of cocaine. The illicit trade, such as it was, remained in the hands of independent drifters; young travelers who rotated through Colombia from El Salvador and Peru, drawn to a good life, which they financed by smuggling into the U.S. small packets of coke, hidden in their luggage or crammed uncomfortably into various body orifices.

Today, fifty years on, more cocaine is being produced and trafficked than ever before. Thanks to prohibition, more Americans have criminal records than university degrees. In Colombia, an actual war, funded almost exclusively by the profits of the drug trade, left 400,000 dead and seven million internally displaced; in the past five decades, millions more have abandoned the country, some by choice, others desperate to escape.

Cocaine has been Colombia's curse, but the engine driving the trade has always been consumption. The cartels rose out of the barrios and country clubs of Medellín and Cali, but the ultimate responsibility for Colombia's agonies lies in good measure with every person who has ever bought street cocaine and every foreign nation that has made possible the illicit market by prohibiting the drug without curbing its use in any serious way.

Even were the complete removal of the plant to be desirable, it's highly unlikely that countries like Colombia and Peru could ever eliminate the cultivation of coca. The financial incentives for small family farmers are too great and the potential growing areas too vast and inaccessible, especially in the ecological and altitudinal zones where cultivated coca thrives.

Crop substitution programs are delusional. Coca produces three harvests a year, generating returns that dwarf those of any other crop. Aerial eradication is doomed to failure, even as it compromises pristine forests and taints the soil and waterways with toxins. Juan Manuel Santos, the 2016 Nobel Laureate for Peace, served as minister of defense under

Álvaro Uribe and for two terms as Colombia's president. No one in the world, as he suggested in a recent podcast, has been responsible for eliminating more coca plants than him and his government, policies that proved, in his own words, to have been a total failure. Santos now advocates the only rational solution: the cleansing stroke of legalization, without which the corrosive influence of cocaine will never subside.

The War on Drugs has not only been a grotesque failure, it has blackened the name and robbed us of the promise of one of the most beneficial plants known to botanical science. When, in the 1970s, Weil and Plowman attempted to develop coca-based products that had the potential to wean Americans from their addictions to coffee and tobacco, they were shut down by a government hell-bent on the pursuit of egregious policies that have only made a bad situation worse with each passing year. In her classic book *The March of Folly*, the historian Barbara Tuchman defined *folly* as the acts of political leaders who, though in full possession of the facts, nevertheless pursue policies contrary to the best interests of their people and nations. By any objective measure, the War on Drugs has been the most misguided crusade in the history of public policy, save perhaps for the actual Crusades, and we all know how they ended. Yet the drug war goes on, month after month, decade after decade, with no one held accountable for its failures, and no end in sight.

We remain stuck for a simple reason, something I came to understand many years ago, soon after I returned from South America in 1975. There was a position advertised at the USDA that Tim Plowman wanted me to apply for, though he warned that if I took the job, he'd kill me. Intrigued, I went out to the USDA campus in Beltsville, Maryland, and found

·my way to the office of a corpulent bureaucrat who clearly was no agricultural agent. He was Drug Enforcement Administration, head to toe.

The first thing I noticed was that he was an addict; I could hardly see across the room for the cigarette smoke. The shelves of his bookcases were cluttered with drug paraphernalia. It was like going into the office of an anti-pornographer and finding the walls papered with pornography. The man was wearing a bright orange jacket over a shirt with a wide butterfly collar that showed off a hairy chest. The hair was red. Around his neck were gold chains; his wristwatch had small nuggets of gold on the band. It was soon clear that all he had gleaned from our research was that Tim and I were good at finding coca fields. The job description called for me to return to Peru to collect any organism—insect, fungus, mold—that attacked and caused damage to coca plants. I was to bring them back to the lab so they could be genetically manipulated and then reintroduced, presumably with more lethal capabilities. When I suggested that this might be a somewhat hazardous assignment, he stuck his hand under his shirt and brought out a gold dog tag, inscribed with the names of field agents he had lost.

As the interview came to an end, I realized that although we had never met before, I knew him well. In the early 1970s, I crossed paths in Medellín with many who later made their names in the drug business, and if the future of the trade remained unclear at the time, the dark essence of these men and women was more than evident.

As I left the office at Beltsville, I understood in a heartbeat that the man asking me to manipulate nature in order to destroy coca was cut from exactly the same cloth as those making fortunes smuggling cocaine. Energetically, they were one and the same, two sides of the same coin: the DEA and the anti-drug crusaders, and the cartels and all of their *sicarios*. Neither had the slightest interest in ending the War on Drugs. The drug traffickers would see their empires implode, with profits plummeting. Interest in cocaine—a shitty drug—might well fade to nothing once the scent of money was removed from the scene.

As for those in the DEA, a victorious end to their obsessive war would find them all out on the streets, looking for work. As long as they can maintain the folly, with enemies to pursue, their appropriation is the safest in the U.S. federal budget, garnering support from every branch of the bureaucracy because virtually every agency has a piece of that $50-billion pie. For this reason alone, the War on Drugs will never be won, for ending it is not in the interests of either side.

Needless to say, I didn't take that job, but apparently someone did. Twenty-five years after Tim Plowman, working for the USDA, revealed coca to be a mild and benign stimulant, essential to the diet, culture, and spiritual life of Andean and Amazonian peoples, the U.S. approved the use of a novel fungus, *Fusarium oxysporum*, developed by scientists at the USDA with the specific goal of wiping out coca wherever the plant was found. They also experimented with a moth, *Eloria noyesi*, known throughout the Amazon as the *gringo* because of its insatiable appetite for coca. In the end, much to the disappointment of the DEA, the scheme was canceled by Bill Clinton, who was concerned that the unilateral use of such agents would be perceived diplomatically, especially in Latin America, to be a form of biological warfare, which, of course, it was.

Frustrated on one front, those dead set on eradicating coca turned to defoliants. Beginning in 1990, and continuing for more than two decades, U.S. contractors in Colombia sprayed glyphosate, commonly known as Roundup, over 4.4 million acres of fields and surrounding forest. The herbicide kills plant life indiscriminately, leaving the forests, in the words of Colombian botanist Alberto Gómez, "burnt to ashes."

Gómez worked seven years on the eradication campaign but came away disillusioned, convinced that little was accomplished by aerial fumigation save the destruction of the wild and the violation of local people who, faced with hunger in the ruin of their gardens, readily turned against the state. If sprayed, he reported, coca fields were immediately harvested and the crop salvaged. In time, all such lands could be replanted, and most were. The impact on cocaine production was negligible. The acreage dedicated to coca in Colombia grew steadily each year through 2007, and then, even as eradication efforts began to be felt in some regions, overall declines in production were offset by increases in productivity in the healthy fields.

In 2015, Juan Manuel Santos, then president, suspended the program out of concern for the health of the nation's children; it was reported that in some Indigenous communities, 80 percent of children exposed to aerial spraying had fallen sick with skin rashes, fever, diarrhea, and eye infections. If not replanted, every acre of coca destroyed only forced growers deeper into the pristine forests of the Amazon, resulting in soaring rates of deforestation.

In 2019, cocaine production in Colombia reached an all-time high, only to increase again in 2020. Even as the country struggled with the biggest humanitarian crisis in the history of the hemisphere, offering food, housing, medical care, schooling, and the right to work to two million Venezuelan refugees, the U.S. government threatened to revoke more than half a billion dollars in foreign aid if the Colombian government did not resume aerial spraying with glyphosate, despite a 2014 WHO report suggesting that the defoliant may be carcinogenic. President Iván Duque agreed to resume spraying, making Colombia the only Latin American nation willing to tolerate the presence of American contractors fully intent on saturating the air and soils of the nation with chemicals designed to kill everything green that grows. "The drug war has tried in vain to keep cocaine out of people's noses," remarked Sanho Tree, director of the Drug Policy Project at the Institute for Policy Studies, "but could result instead in scorching the lungs of the Earth."

SURELY, IT IS TIME to find another way. Rather than yielding to American pressure to expand the aerial use of herbicides, it's not unreasonable to ask why any of Colombia's biodiversity, perhaps its greatest national asset, not to mention the health and well-being of its children, should be put at risk to satisfy the misguided policies of a foreign country. Having endured the consequences of the illicit trade for so many years, perhaps now is the time for Colombia to reclaim a stolen legacy by celebrating coca for what it really is, what the Inca saw it to be.

Marketed as a tea, perhaps as a chewing gum for those not keen on dried or powdered leaves, the sacred plant could be Colombia's greatest gift to the world, dwarfing the commercial success of coffee, in good measure because coca is simply a better product. Who would not want to experience a sense of enhanced energy and mental clarity, a mild suppression of hunger, a gentle feeling of creative confidence, a lightness to one's step lasting throughout the day, knowing that the source of your slight elevation of mood was a benign and highly nutritious leaf that has been revered by the peoples and ancient civilizations of South America for five thousand years?

In a digital economy in which work for so many implies long hours staring at a screen, what could be more welcome or promising than a natural product that facilitates focus and concentration, even while inducing a subtle sense of contentment and well-being? Coca is the ideal companion for any creative endeavor, be it writing poetry or code, composing music, or simply basking in the silence of the stars.

Those who experience coca invariably come away astonished by its subtle yet pleasant effects and its practical use. Coca works, and it works for everyone, in idiosyncratic ways. In my case, a writer happily cursed with a frenetic travel schedule, coca allows me take a seat on an airplane after a busy day and return immediately to the task at hand, picking up right where I left off in a text, watching as the words flow from my fingers, oblivious to all distractions.

At the moment, coca is listed in Schedule II of the U.S. federal Controlled Substances Act, a category reserved for drugs with acknowledged therapeutic use but also a high potential for abuse. Technically, physicians can prescribe coca, as Andrew Weil has written, but in practice they can't, for there is no legal source and the therapeutic indications have not formally been specified. Marijuana, by contrast, along with ecstasy, mescaline, and LSD have long been listed

in Schedule I, classified as drugs with serious abuse potential but no recognized medical applications; drugs in this
category are deemed to be the most dangerous, the greatest
threats to society. And yet today, even as Canada and forty
other nations have legalized the use of cannabis, and hallu-
cinogens are being heralded as the therapeutic instruments
of a psychedelic renaissance that will transform the treatment of mental health, coca, despite its long history as a
healing plant, remains off-limits, simply because of its association with the cocaine trade.

This has to change. Some weeks ago, I called Andy Weil.
We hadn't been in touch for some time, and yet it felt as if
we had never been apart. Our thoughts turned, as they often
have over the years, to memories of our long-departed friend,
Tim Plowman, who died in 1989. Tim had devoted his professional life to the study of coca—the plant had no greater
champion—only to have his research, the result of years
of botanical exploration in the most difficult and remote
reaches of a continent, denied and betrayed by the very government that had sponsored his work. Andy and I decided to
once again take up the cause of this sacred plant, if only to
expose the folly of those who have kept Tim's dreams from
being realized, even while promoting policies that have only
brought violence, corruption, and pain to the world.

Our mission is to stimulate research that will document
coca's medical and therapeutic benefits, with the goal of making available for all people a plant that promises to improve
their well-being and ease the day-to-day challenges of their
lives. A wide array of coca-based products will bring delight
to consumers, even while supporting the 130,000 Colombian families who grow the plant for a living, allowing them
to sever their ties to the cartels. The liberation of the leaves

will undermine the black-market trade and reduce deforestation by opening up for cultivation lands long ago cleared and abandoned. Through taxation, it will generate revenues for Colombia that will allow a long-suffering nation to pay the price of peace, having drained its treasury for fifty years to cover the costs of a war only made possible by the sordid profits of prohibition.

We are not alone in this quest. Colombia is on side with the plant, as are the people of Peru and those of Bolivia who are sick and tired of their patrimony being denied, their gift to the world insulted and refused. Throughout Andean South America, there are scores of new enterprises, all focused on the beneficial potential of the leaves as food, medicine, stimulant, and sacrament.

A new generation of political leadership in Latin America has found the courage to defy American pressure, setting their nations on new paths that will bring an end to policies that have only served the interests of criminals, profiteers, and state institutions with a vested interest in prosecuting their War on Drugs indefinitely, no matter the consequences.

Within weeks of his inauguration in 2022, Gustavo Petro, president of Colombia, made good on his campaign promise to end the forced eradication of coca. He is on record as supporting legislation that will decriminalize and regulate cocaine sales. The president has taken such a stand not because he endorses the use of the drug, but because he knows that only by destroying the illicit trade, and the profits that fuel it, will it be possible to secure peace, stability, and prosperity for the Colombian people.

Should President Petro succeed, undercutting the black market with the cleansing stroke of legalization, even while bringing the gift of coca to the world, he will both inspire his supporters and give pause to his opponents, those who view his young presidency across a chasm of uncertainty and trepidation. What better way to signal a new beginning for all of Colombia, a nation divided but a people long united in hope, resilience, and faith. An end at last to the War on Drugs. A stolen legacy returned to its rightful status. A sacred plant, long defiled, heralded, as in the time of the Inca and all the ancient civilizations of the Andes, as a gift of the gods: coca, the divine leaf of immortality.

11

BEYOND CLIMATE FEAR
AND TREPIDATION

I WAS NOT IN GLASGOW in 2021 as 120 world leaders, 40,000 official participants, 3,886 journalists, and several thousand activists converged on the city for COP26, the UN Climate Change Conference that famously ended in disappointment. But I was in Edinburgh a year later as scores of rugby fans filled airport bars at five in the morning, overwhelming ordinary tourists, whose numbers alone were more than sufficient to signal the return of mass travel in the wake of the COVID pandemic. Posters and digital displays at every turn proclaimed the airport authority's commitment to a carbon-free future, a goal that in the moment was surely the last thing on the minds of those dressed colorfully for the game, swilling beer, about to fly off in support of their team.

However dire the prognosis, people get on with their lives. In the summer of 2022, even as temperatures soared to record highs in England, with wildfires scorching France, a *New York Times*/Siena College poll determined that just 1 percent of American voters considered climate change the most important issue facing the country; among citizens under thirty, the generation most alarmed by the crisis, that number rose to a mere 3 percent. A litany of immediate concerns trumped climate: inflation, the price of gas, rising interest rates, the political divide tearing at the nation. What counts for most is the present, not a threat that, despite all evidence of a warming world, remains for many a problem of the future.

Climate science is a rarefied discipline, based on mathematical and statistical models of bewildering complexity. But one need not be a climate expert to be haunted by the disconnect between the severity of the threat as proclaimed every day in the media and the global community's actual response as measured not in words but in action and deed. There is a chasm between those who derive purpose and identity from the climate crisis and those for whom the crisis appears to have neither relevance nor meaning. Something is not working. Understanding why the message is not getting through—or, better said, why it has failed to set in motion a global response equal to the danger at hand—takes on greater urgency with each passing day.

With the climate community having recently convened in Dubai for the latest UN Climate Change Conference, the twenty-eighth to be held since global warming was identified as an existential threat at Stockholm in 1972, it's an opportune moment to take a critical look at both the message and the messengers, if only to seek a more effective way forward. Any deviation from the climate consensus invites controversy. But, as my good friend the late Tom Lovejoy, who coined the term biodiversity, once remarked, what's the point of having a reputation if you are not prepared to spend it? As much as anyone, I acknowledge the climate crisis as the defining challenge of our times. But I also recognize that realism is not apathy, and rhetoric no substitute for results. If the global energy grid is to be transformed, we must be prepared to look beneath the surface of things to see where we are, where we need to be, and what may be holding us back as we confront a peril unprecedented in the human experience.

SOME WEEKS BEFORE COP15, the UN Climate Change Conference in Copenhagen in December 2009, I was hired by TBWA, the international advertising agency, as part of its effort to promote the launch of the Leaf, Nissan's foray into the electric car market. The company sent me to Copenhagen with two film crews and a demanding list of deliverables—daily blog posts, stand-up reports and commentaries, interviews for YouTube, and tweets—but complete freedom to report on the conference as I saw fit. The car itself was not to be mentioned; the marketing strategy was to promote not the vehicle but the need for it, given the looming climate crisis.

The assignment introduced me to the culture of climate action at a global event that had been widely heralded as a fulcrum of history, a point of no return. A sense of urgency infused both the conference halls and the city streets, where representatives of environmental groups from all corners of the world, unable to secure a place among the formal delegates, gathered by the thousands.

The scene in the streets of Copenhagen was hopeful and exhilarating. But as COP15 ended, it left many who were there both discouraged and perplexed. If the fate of the world hung in the balance, if rising sea levels promised to flood the Nile delta and inundate the homes of 120 million people in Bangladesh and India, if nearly half the world would be forced to live without access to potable water, if the glaciers of the

Andes and all the Tibetan Plateau were to be gone within our lifetimes, why was our response so feeble?

According to Rajendra Pachauri, then chair of the UN Intergovernmental Panel on Climate Change (the IPCC), the climate crisis could be mitigated and the world transformed with an investment equivalent to just 3 percent of the global economy. The United States alone devoted 40 percent of GDP to military victory in World War II. Why had we not mobilized and declared war on global warming?

As every voice at COP15 affirmed, the science on climate was unequivocal, the threat both extreme and immediate, and the solutions were at hand, if only politicians had the will to act. Transitioning from fossil fuels to wind, solar, and other renewable energy sources would both save the planet and generate a massive economic stimulus as thousands of "green" jobs came online to serve the needs of a trans-formed economy. This was the core message of Copenhagen, a climate narrative seductive in its simplicity that would, in time, be codified as the Green New Deal, celebrated as a new paradigm, a road map to a carbon-free world inspired and informed by economic justice and ecological sustainability.

And yet, as I flew back to Washington, D.C., surrounded in first class by climate luminaries, all COP15 attendees and all veterans of any number of previous UN global confer-ences, a few things didn't add up. For one, I was troubled by the consistency of the climate narrative, both from those I interviewed and more particularly from the twenty or more books that I'd read in prepping for the assignment. The books, whether written by journalists, climate scientists, or activists, all shared the same narrative thread, the same citations, the same arguments.

The official multilateral scene in Copenhagen had not inspired confidence. The major industrial nations glossed and exaggerated the significance of their emission reduction plans, while countries of the global south, as well as Saudi Arabia, grew ever more insistent in their demands for compensation. The African nations spoke of reparations. The European Union, in a transparently disingenuous gesture, promised 20 percent reductions, with the chance for more, knowing full well that a 12 percent drop had already been achieved since 1990, the benchmark year, with the admission of a dozen feeble industrial economies of the former Soviet Bloc.

China offered to reduce its carbon intensity, a rhetorical sleight of hand that would allow absolute emissions to rise, provided they did not surpass the surge of industrial growth that has condemned 400,000 Chinese to die each year from toxic air. India effectively stated that having been slow to industrialize, it was now its turn to poison the world. The fact that we are all in this together, that there is only one planet, and that we all must find a way to take collective responsibility for this moment in time seemed utterly lost on the formal delegations.

Copenhagen also demonstrated the extent to which the climate issue, even then, had consumed the energy, attention, and resources of the global environmental movement. Every environmental group in the world, or so it seemed, had a presence in the city, though very few had an actual role to play or any reason to attend. The real work of protecting local forests, rivers, and lakes—the natural capital of home—had in so many places been set aside as environmental activists and professionals pursued the holy grail of climate, a target so abstract that no individual or organization needed to worry about accountability, let alone the risks and discomforts of political action or confrontation.

The conference went on for a week, and yet, in all the talk, there was one omission so glaring as to call into question the seriousness of the entire endeavor. Only a campaign focused on activity rather than results could expunge from all consideration the one fuel that can get us from where we are to where we want to be, from an economy based on carbon to one fired by the renewable energy of the sun. Surely any discussion about a carbon-free future had to consider the nuclear option, an energy source that has met, for example, 70 percent of France's electricity needs since 1974, even while generating for the country over $3 billion a year in export revenues.

As Stewart Brand has written, nuclear may be a problem when things go terribly wrong, but fossil fuels are a problem when things go exactly as planned. If carbon is an existential threat, as speaker after speaker at COP15 proclaimed, then surely nuclear is a bridge that cannot be categorically ignored. But at Copenhagen, it most assuredly was, as if but a toxic artifact of the past.

Consider, as an aside, Pacific Gas and Electric's recent plan, now suspended, to shut down Diablo Canyon, California's last nuclear plant, which generates 9 percent of the state's energy. In 2012, when California closed the nuclear plant at San Onofre, the state was forced to turn to natural gas; in terms of carbon emissions, it was the equivalent of putting two million additional cars on the road.

IN 2014, FIVE YEARS AFTER COP15, Steven Koonin, undersecretary for science in the U.S. Department of Energy under President Obama, published an op-ed in the Wall

Street Journal suggesting that the science on climate was by no means settled and that we were, in fact, a long way from possessing the knowledge needed to devise good climate policies. Conventional thinking, driven largely by the media and advocates with no ability to assess the scientific literature, was, he argued, dangerously distorting policy debates on all issues related to energy, carbon emissions, and the environment.

The climate, Koonin agreed, is changing; it always has and always will. In the twentieth century, the Earth's global average surface temperature rose 1.4 degrees Fahrenheit (0.8 degrees Celsius). And, without doubt, humans are influencing the climate through the emissions of greenhouse gases, largely through the burning of fossil fuels. The effects of carbon dioxide will persist for centuries. But the key question is this: How will the climate change over the next century under both natural and human influences? Answering this question, Koonin noted, is both critical and far more difficult than many assume.

By the middle of the twenty-first century, anthropogenic additions of carbon dioxide are expected to shift the atmosphere's natural greenhouse effect by 1 to 2 percent. Given the variability of climate systems, this modest figure, Koonin argued, makes it very difficult to project with confidence the consequences of human activities alone. The models that are the source of climate predictions, he added, are not precise. In science, one can ask complex questions of simple systems or simple questions of complex systems. Computer modeling of complex systems "is as much an art as a science."

Koonin also noted the fundamental role of oceans, influences that play out on a time scale measured in centuries. Comprehensive observations of what happens in the open seas have only been available to science for the last few decades. By the same token, the impact of feedback dynamics, whether they amplify or mute various trends, cannot be determined confidently from the laws of physics and chemistry alone; they must be verified by precise, detailed observations that are, in many cases, not yet available.

The international authority on climate is the UN Intergovernmental Panel on Climate Change, which since 1990 has periodically surveyed the state of climate science, reviewing literally thousands of technical documents and academic papers. These reports are considered the definitive assessment of climate science at the time of their issue. Intended for policymakers and politicians, the language of the summaries distilled from these massive documents—the latest, AR6, released August 9, 2021, contained 3,949 pages—cannot be expected to reflect all the complexities of the original research. But the challenge comes when, to capture the attention of the nonscientist, conclusions and declarations suggest a precision and certainty that the science, and indeed the review process itself, may not support.

Any honest conversation, Koonin noted, must begin by acknowledging not only the scientific certainties but also the uncertainties. Proposals for mitigation, for example, should not imply that the profound changes demanded by a carbon-free world will not come at a cost. Climate is an overriding concern, but any sweeping policy prescription must also consider other societal priorities—economic development, poverty reduction, global health, intergenerational and geographical equity. Misrepresenting the current state of climate science, he concluded, will not help us address humanity's deepest needs and desires.

What came across as a provocative but well-reasoned argument was received by the climate community as if heresy; Koonin was attacked not just for what he said but for having said it. Some demanded that he be fired from his academic post, with little consideration given to his unassailable credentials—professor of theoretical physics at Caltech, member of the U.S. Academy of Sciences and the American Academy of Arts and Science, independent governor of the Lawrence Livermore National Laboratory, author of more than two hundred peer-reviewed papers in the fields of physics and astrophysics, scientific computation, energy technology and policy, and climate science. As undersecretary for science in Obama's Department of Energy, Koonin had been responsible for determining and prioritizing actions on both the local and national level that would most effectively reduce carbon emissions.

In the summer of 2021, quite by chance, I heard Professor Koonin speak at a literary festival in northern California. His presentation was free of judgments or polemics. He came across as neither contrarian nor iconoclast but as a serious and thoughtful scientist, properly skeptical of any orthodoxy and fully aware of the costs and consequences of implementing public policy initiatives on a global scale. His book *Unsettled: What Climate Science Tells Us, What It Doesn't, and Why It Matters* was as steady as his presentation.

Not for an instant does Koonin deny that anthropogenic carbon emissions are rising or that the climate is changing. On the contrary, he questions nothing, save our reflexive faith in definitive assessments that the data may not actually confirm or support. Not that the data are necessarily wrong or distorted; the challenge is complex, and the answers not always simple or clear. Koonin's attitude was that of a scientist, confident in what is known and humble enough to accept what remains unknown, perhaps even unknowable, for the moment. Before nations spend trillions of dollars, we need to ask whether such expenditures will make a difference. This did not strike me as being unreasonable.

I went online only to learn that Koonin had been pilloried, often in an ad hominem way. Merely to raise concerns, it seems, is to be branded a climate denier and marginalized by the scientific community. I found this disturbing. Between the actual deniers driven by ideology or cynically serving the interests of industry and the prophets of doom who have an almost biblical obsession with the coming apocalypse, there are scientists like Koonin, as well as professionals in other fields, whose voices are not being considered, at least in part because they pose awkward questions. I set out to hear what they had to say.

And what I heard over several months was a sobering assessment of the promise and complexity of the challenge before us, a message both daunting and oddly invigorating in its clarity and realism. There is a way forward, pragmatic and hopeful, that offers a positive vision certain to quell our most debilitating fears and restore open and critical dialogue to the global conversation, even while rallying governments and citizens to action, all with the goal of making real the transformation that we seek and that the climate crisis demands.

AMONG THE MOST CONTROVERSIAL of these voices is that of the Danish political scientist Bjorn Lomborg, author of *Cool It* (2007) and *False Alarm* (2020), books that, as the titles suggest, approach the issue of climate change from the perspective one might expect of a young man who shot to fame in 2001 with the publication of *The Skeptical Environmentalist*. In questioning the climate consensus, Lomborg, a visiting fellow at Stanford's Hoover Institution, has long been a lightning rod, attracting the ire of those deeply invested in the very orthodoxy that he addresses. He has been dismissed as a "closet climate denier," and critics invariably note that he has no formal training as a climate scientist, which is true of both him and any number of prominent climate activists. Others have accused him of cherry-picking the data, ignoring facts that contradict or fail to serve his arguments. Lamentably, it's a practice not uncommon in the climate community.

Lomborg's sweeping analysis, to be sure, is not without flaws; notable, according to some critics, is his failure to factor into economic assessments the direct and indirect subsidies of the fossil fuel industry. But if Lomborg's research is all "political propaganda," as one reviewer has railed, it is seen as such largely because he dares critique the orthodoxy. Rajendra Pachauri, when chair of the IPCC, rather hysterically compared Lomborg to Adolf Hitler.

Despite the opposition of those who consider his views heretical, Lomborg's message resonates with many because it makes sense to ordinary people. He may be wrong, for example, about a specific cost estimate, but not in his fundamental assertion that the transformation of the global energy infrastructure will involve enormous expenditures and massive transfers of wealth from individuals to governments and from nations to nations. He is certainly not wrong in casting a sharp eye on questions of compliance, efficacy, the role of the media, or the impact of apocalyptic pronouncements on the hopes and dreams of the young in all nations. And he is not misguided in his assessment of the scale of the challenge before us, as we transition to a new energy future, the features of which remain only partially known, save the certainty that global demand for power will increase by at least 50 percent by the year 2050.

Like it or not, we are a fossil fuel civilization. For three hundred years, we have consumed the ancient sunlight of the world. Currently, we burn more than ten billion tons of carbon-based fuels a year. Since the first international climate meeting in 1992, thirty-odd years ago, the world has only managed to reduce dependency on fossil fuels from 87 to 83 percent of our energy needs. To suggest that in another thirty years, by 2050, even as the world economy doubles to $185 trillion, we'll be able to transition from 83 percent to zero is an act of faith.

To be sure, remarkable progress has been made. In just the last decade, the cost of solar power and lithium-battery technology has fallen by more than 85 percent, the cost of wind power by more than 55 percent. Investments in green energy now surpass those in fossil fuels, a market shift few could have anticipated as recently as 2009, when delegates gathered in Copenhagen for COP15.

Still, there is a very long way to go. Between 1995 and 2018, years that saw massive government subsidies for solar and wind generation, the share of global energy production derived from zero-emission sources grew by just two percentage points, reaching 15 percent. In 2021, renewable energy sources accounted for only 12 percent of total U.S. energy needs.

A study conducted by Finland's Geological Society, published in 2021, concluded that to replace the 46,423 power stations currently operating worldwide on oil, coal, gas, and nuclear energy would require the construction of 586,000 power stations run by wind, solar, and hydrogen. According to the World Bank, as reported by Christopher Pollon, over three billion tons of minerals and metals will be needed by 2050 to build the infrastructure necessary to store and deploy renewable energy on a global scale.

Norway recently launched the first electric container ship. It can carry 120 containers, with a range of about 30 nautical miles. The biggest conventional ship in the world carries 24,000 containers, with a range of 13,000 nautical miles.

The total battery capacity currently available in the entire United States could electrify the nation for all of fourteen seconds. Tesla's $5-billion Gigafactory in Nevada will be the world's largest manufacturing facility for lithium batteries; its projected annual production, if taken as a whole, could handle perhaps three minutes of the nation's electrical demands.

Storage capacity aside, there is the problem of moving the power to market. Establishing a new grid of transmission lines to get the power generated by wind and solar installations to the consumer is not trivial, given the opposition of those who may celebrate renewable energy provided the wind farms, solar fields, and transmission lines do not blemish their own communities. A 2021 survey, conducted by the University of Georgia and published in *The Energy Journal*, found that only 24 percent of Americans were willing to live within a mile of a solar field; a mere 17 percent would tolerate a wind farm so close to their homes.

Consider as but one example the TransWest Express, a $3-billion power line conceived to bring renewable energy from a wind farm in Wyoming to two million customers in the American Southwest. The proponents, according to *Bloomberg*, "spent years lining up hundreds of permits and easements from local governments and landowners along the route." They secured all but one: Cross Mountain Ranch did not want its pristine Colorado landscape marred by power lines. Seventeen years after the start of the project, not a single wire has been strung.

In 2017, the residents of Cape Cod, among them several nationally known environmental advocates, defeated plans for a 130-turbine wind farm after the developer had invested $100 million in the project. In the wake of that decision, wind developers adopted the Starbucks rule: no project would be considered unless situated at least thirty miles away from the nearest Starbucks; those comfortable with paying five dollars for a cup of coffee included too many certain to oppose any new infrastructure in their neighborhoods.

After twenty years of government subsidies, there are about seven million electric vehicles on the road. Throughout the world, some 1.5 billion internal combustion vehicles remain in service. Flip these figures and then tally the investment of time and money necessary to transform the global transportation infrastructure. In the United States alone, there are some 150,000 gas stations. The number in China exceeds 100,000 and is growing. Replace these with charging stations. Factor in supply chains and the political and economic implications of a global competition for rare metals, cobalt and lithium in particular. Consider the environmental consequences of a soaring demand for copper; electric cars require three times as much as traditional gas-driven vehicles. Consumption of nickel, largely for truck and car batteries, is expected to increase fourfold by 2050.

In making these calculations, note that about a fifth of an electric car is made of plastic, derived from fossil fuels. Recall, too, that nearly half of its carbon footprint comes about long before it hits the road; emissions resulting from the production of electric vehicles are nearly 70 percent higher than those generated in the manufacture of gas-fueled cars, their toxicity index three times as much, due to the greater use of heavy metals. Over twenty years, a conventional car in both its manufacture and operative life accounts for around twenty-four tons of carbon dioxide; an electric vehicle of the same size about nineteen tons. Changing the energy source from gasoline to electricity addresses less than 25 percent of a vehicle's total carbon footprint. And if the electricity used to charge a domestic fleet is generated by power plants still fired by coal or natural gas, as will certainly be the case in much of India and China for some time to come, the promise of a transformation deemed by so many to be essential to the future of the planet may remain unrealized. Going electric is surely a good thing, but so is a realistic assessment of what such a societal investment will accomplish.

At COP26 in Glasgow in 2021, President Biden implored world leaders to stop burning fossil fuels. His signature legislative initiative budgeted $555 billion to address the crisis. He declared climate change to be an "existential threat to human existence as we know it." And yet, according to the Center for Biological Diversity, the Biden administration in its first year approved 3,557 permits for oil and gas drilling, 899 more than were granted in the initial twelve months of a presidency led by Donald Trump, an unabashed climate change denier. As gasoline prices surged in the summer of 2021, Biden called on Saudi Arabia to increase production;

within days of returning from Scotland, his administration auctioned off eighty million acres in the Gulf of Mexico for offshore drilling.

In 2022, as John Kerry, Biden's leading voice on climate, warned African nations of the risks to the planet should they develop their fossil fuel resources, the United States dramatically expanded its own carbon-based energy sector, approving developments and issuing permits on a scale unequaled by any other nation. The Willow project in Alaska, authorized by Biden in 2023, is expected to yield 600 million barrels of oil. Burned as fuel, this oil will add 9.2 million metric tons of carbon dioxide to the atmosphere every year, equivalent to the emissions of two million gasoline cars. A huge number, but still just a fifth of 1 percent of America's total carbon emissions. In 2023, even as John Kerry circled the globe sharing his conservation message, the United States, already the world's largest producer of oil and the third-largest consumer of coal, became the biggest exporter of natural gas.

There is a chasm between rhetoric and reality, which is only deepened by the voices of public advocates and activists who have, no doubt with the best of intentions, infused the climate movement with the moral authority of a millenarian crusade. Al Gore, who has deservedly earned the highest accolades for his public stand, has described the climate crisis as "a generational mission, a moral purpose, the opportunity to … experience an epiphany as we discover that this crisis is not about politics at all … It is a moral and spiritual challenge … At stake is the survival of our civilization and the habitability of the Earth."

In 2006, Gore declared that within ten years, the world would reach a point of no return. In 2009, he said that the entire polar ice cap would most likely melt away by 2014. In 2019, the Prince of Wales, today King Charles III, gave us eighteen months to get things right. With the release in 2021 of the latest UN scientific assessment, AR6, Secretary-General António Guterres declared a "code red for humanity," warning that billions of people were at immediate risk. "Before this century is over," affirmed James Lovelock, "billions of us will die and the few breeding pairs of people that survive will be in the Arctic where the climate remains tolerable."

In the face of such ominous predictions, climate activists feel a moral obligation to alert the world, even if it invokes the apocalyptic, exaggerates the threat, and fails to acknowledge uncertainty or doubt. As Stanford's Stephen Schneider conceded, "We need to get some broad-based support, to capture the public's imagination. That, of course, entails getting loads of media coverage. So, we offer up scary scenarios, make simplified, dramatic statements, and make little mention of any doubts we might have."

Like many advocates, Gore has little patience with anyone who questions the climate consensus. "Fifteen percent of the population," he once said, "believe the moon landing was actually staged in a movie lot in Arizona, and somewhat fewer still believe the Earth is flat. I think they all get together with the global warming deniers on a Saturday night and party."

Those who make a personal fetish of climate denial, conflating opinion with facts, anger and indignation with knowledge, distortions with the truth, are surely deserving of Gore's contempt. But a confluence of self-interest also exists among those deeply invested in the unfolding carbon crisis: politicians and the media, climate professionals

and activists, the many business entities that stand to benefit from costly climate policies—manufacturers of electric
vehicles, for example, including Nissan, whose ad campaign
for the Leaf brought me to Copenhagen—not to mention, as
Andrew Cockburn reports in *Harper's Magazine*, the nascent
nuclear industry.

Adhering to the consensus is just part of the culture of
climate science, according to Patrick Brown, codirector of the
climate and energy team at the Breakthrough Institute; it's
the only way for a young academic to get ahead. In August
2023, Brown and six colleagues, all climate specialists, published their research in *Nature*, arguably the world's most
prestigious scientific journal. Their paper focused exclusively
on how warming temperatures have increased the risk, danger, and frequency of extreme wildfires in California. The
story was immediately picked up by the *Los Angeles Times*,
NPR, and other media outlets. Although Brown and his co-
authors were acutely aware that other factors beyond climate
change were involved, they stuck with the storyline journal
editors expected to hear. What appeared in *Nature* was good
science, Brown affirms, but incomplete.

Brown came clean in a subsequent op-ed, "I Left Out the
Full Truth to Get My Climate Change Paper Published," in
The Free Press on September 12, 2023. He began by acknowledging that university researchers frequently tailor their
studies to maximize the likelihood that their work is accepted
by prestigious scientific journals. "I know this," Brown writes,
"because I am one of them. Here's how it works."

The first thing the astute climate researcher knows is that
his or her work should support the mainstream narrative—namely, that the effects of climate change are both

pervasive and catastrophic and that the primary way
to deal with them is not by employing practical adaptation measures...but through policies aimed at reducing
greenhouse gas emissions.

I knew *not* to try to quantify key aspects other than
climate change in my research because it would dilute
the story that journals like *Nature* and *Science* want to
tell. Editors have made it abundantly clear, both by what
they publish and what they reject, that they want climate
papers that support certain preapproved narratives—
even when those narratives come at the expense of
broader knowledge for society.

Climate science has become less about understanding
the complexities of the world and more about serving as a
kind of Cassandra, urgently warning the public about the
dangers of climate change. However understandable this
instinct may be, it distorts a great deal of climate science
research, misinforms the public, and most importantly,
makes practical solutions more difficult to achieve.

What he experienced, Brown suggests, is the norm for
high-profile research publications. He cites, for example,
another influential paper in *Nature* in which scientists determined that the two largest effects of climate change on
society are deaths due to extreme heat and damage to agriculture. In a narrow sense, this may be true, as the paper
demonstrated. Left out of the story is the fact that climate
change is not the dominant factor in either of these impacts:
heat-related deaths have been declining and crop yields
have been increasing for decades *despite* climate change, all
of which is good news and worthy of study, if only to understand how we might overcome the negative effects of a

changing climate. "But studying solutions," as Brown notes, "rather than focusing on problems is simply not going to rouse the public or the press."

Not surprisingly, the language of doom has brought many to the point of despair. A survey reported in *The Lancet* of ten thousand young adults aged sixteen to twenty-five from nineteen nations found over half to be despondent daily, haunted by the specter of climate change. Three out of four characterized the future as "frightening"; 56 percent predicted that climate change will end the human race. In 2020, a large national survey in the U.K. found that one in five British children were having nightmares about climate change. In another poll, fully a third of American adults under age forty-five expressed reluctance to have children, fearful of what the future will bring.

In 2017, the American Psychological Association diagnosed rising eco-anxiety as a syndrome, characterized by "a chronic fear of environmental doom." A 2019 *Washington Post* survey of teenagers thirteen to seventeen years old found over half feeling sad, anxious, angry, helpless, and guilty, again because of what they had heard about the climate crisis. Significantly, when asked the source of their information, more than 70 percent cited television, news, and movies. This finding suggests a critical dynamic. What the public knows of the climate crisis, it learns from the media, the last filter in a long game of telephone that begins with scientific studies no layperson can understand, moves through a couple of interpretive steps that only a naïf would assume to be totally free of politics and preconceptions, and reaches finally to the media, journalists focused on the next headline, the darker the better, distilled from a story that is infinite in its complexity, with a timeline measured not in hours or days but in centuries and millennia.

Consider, by way of example, Paris and the core commitments that emerged from the 2015 climate conference. Politicians wanted to know what it would take to keep global temperatures from rising more than 1.5 degrees Celsius. Asked to envision the impossible, scientists responded with the impossible, policies that theoretically might achieve that target by 2030 but that, by definition, implied immediate and unprecedented changes to all aspects of society, initiatives that for political, technological, and cultural reasons would never be implemented. The media turned these theoretical recommendations into an existential imperative, allowing CNN to report in 2018, three years after Paris, that the "Earth has twelve years to avert climate change catastrophe."

Such headlines, both factually wrong and ethically questionable, readily become social media memes, codified in digital realms where anonymity and boredom conspire to reinvent the truth. In 2021, John Kerry invoked CNN's distortion when he stated during an interview on CBS, "The scientists told us three years ago we had twelve years to avert the worst consequences of the climate crisis. We are now three years gone, so we have nine years left." As the top U.S. spokesperson on the climate crisis, Kerry's words carried the full weight of a presidency that would declare global warming to be an absolute and certain threat to life as we know it on Earth. Is it any wonder that youth and children are both frightened and angry?

In 2018, even as CNN issued its apocalyptic warning, Greta Thunberg, a student of just fifteen, began a solitary protest outside the Swedish parliament in Stockholm. Her courage and conviction hit a nerve, and she soon rose to global acclaim with a bold call not for mere reductions but for an immediate end to all carbon emissions, a policy that if implemented would imply the cessation of economic activity across much of the world. There was no time to waste. "Around 2030," she affirmed, "we will be in a position to set off an irreversible chain reaction beyond human control that will lead to the end of our civilization as we know it."

With her dark forebodings and quirky activism, Thunberg landed on the cover of *Time*, the magazine's youngest ever Person of the Year. *Forbes* added her to its list of the world's one hundred most powerful women. She has been nominated for the Nobel Peace Prize not once but for three years running. In 2019, her voice reached the U.S. Congress, as Democratic congresswoman Alexandria Ocasio-Cortez shared Thunberg's deepest concern: "The world is going to end in twelve years if we don't address climate change."

Thunberg has inspired millions, mobilizing youth around the world. Her radical prescription for the global economy is less folly, her supporters would say, than the only sane and rational response, given that the Earth faces imminent destruction. Fear fuels her activism. By her own account, she first heard about climate change at age eight and couldn't understand why adults weren't confronting the danger. This led to depression and despair. At eleven, she stopped talking. Avoiding food, she lost twenty-two pounds in two months. In time, Thunberg was diagnosed with Asperger's syndrome, obsessive-compulsive disorder, and selective mutism, challenges that she turned into strengths. But it was not easy. She continued to struggle with depression in the years leading up to 2018 and the protest that brought her to the attention of the world.

Thunberg is today a spokesperson for a generation. With each passing month and year, her rhetoric grows more strident, her anger more stubborn and blunt. In her youthful face, there remains always the image of an innocent child of eight, haunted by fear, certain that the world is coming to an end.

WITH THE HOPES AND FEARS of all children in mind, let's consider just a few of the climate narratives, the stories that keep us awake at night. Many young people, for example, have heard that with the melting ice in the Arctic, polar bears are on the brink of extinction. But it's not quite so simple. Across the vast expanses of the Arctic, there are nineteen distinct populations, thirteen of which are in Canada, home to two-thirds of all polar bears. Of these, eleven are stable or increasing in numbers, thanks in part to the 1973 Agreement on the Conservation of Polar Bears. The graphic video of an emaciated bear that went viral in 2017, attracting an audience of 2.5 billion to the *National Geographic* website, was highly disturbing, but if the condition of all polar bears was comparable, one would not expect their population to be increasing, as it is, across much of the range of the species. This anomaly was resolved when *National Geographic* acknowledged that the videographer had deliberately misrepresented the plight of a diseased and starving bear in order to advance a political agenda. The individual by his own account had set out to secure an image that would "communicate the urgency of climate change." Fully aware that global warming had nothing to do with the bear's condition, *National Geographic* nevertheless published the footage under the headline, "This is what climate change looks like."

Ultimately what matters is whether polar bears, across all the diverse habitats of the Arctic, can eat. Warming trends affect different populations in different ways. Bears living in the highest reaches of the North may starve if the pack ice is so thick that they cannot hunt seals; an increase in open water could make hunting easier. In the southern extent of their range, by contrast, warming trends may or may not be catastrophic. Bears that live in James Bay have thrived through ice-free summers for thousands of years. In Davis Strait, the extent and thickness of sea ice, and the integrity of the floating platforms offshore from which polar bears hunt, have been declining dramatically for years. And yet the bear population there is today more than twice as large as it was forty years ago.

That polar bears are managing today doesn't imply that their future is secure. They are creatures of the ice, and the ice is melting, most dramatically in the Arctic where the warming rate is four times as high as the global average. According to the Geological Survey of Denmark and Greenland, as reported by Bret Stephens in the *New York Times*, Greenland has lost 170 gigatons of ice every year for thirty years, the equivalent of 5,400 tons every second.

Elsewhere in the world, glaciers have been in retreat since the end of the Little Ice Age, a three-hundred-year period of notably cooler temperatures that began in about 1550 and ended with the onset of a warmer climatic period around 1850. When Hemingway published *The Snows of Kilimanjaro* in 1936, the mountain had lost half of its ice surface in the previous half century; dramatic recession had been recorded since 1800. When the British sailed into Alaska's Glacier Bay in 1794, they found their way blocked by a wall of ice four thousand feet thick. By the time the naturalist John

Muir visited in 1879, that glacier had retreated by more than forty miles.

Ultimately, the cause of glacial recession—be it anthropogenic carbon emissions, climatic cycles over the centuries, or a combination of both—matters less than the pressing need to do whatever is necessary to mitigate the effects, both in mountain areas where communities downstream of swollen glacial lakes are in immediate danger and throughout the Arctic where the entire way of life of the Inuit is at risk.

Without doubt, sea levels are rising. As land ice melts, and warmer air temperatures cause ocean water to expand, they will continue to do so, as has been the norm for the past twenty thousand years. The story of the Earth over the last half million years has been one of continental ice sheets ebbing and flowing, glaciers building up over the land for a hundred thousand years, with sea levels dropping as much as four hundred feet before rising again during warmer periods of glacial retreat that generally have lasted about twenty thousand years. During the last interglacial period some 125,000 years ago, sea levels were twenty feet higher than they are today.

We are currently living through another age of glacial recession that began about twelve thousand years ago. In that time, sea levels have risen four hundred feet, as much as five inches a decade until some seven thousand years ago when the rate slowed to about a foot a century, a pace that continued into our modern era. So, the key question is not whether ocean waters are rising, but rather to what extent anthropogenic climate change is augmenting a phenomenon already unfolding on a geological time scale beyond human control. At the end of the day, what matters is the undeniable fact that the sea is rising, by at least a foot a century, perhaps more. Even in the absence of a climate threat, adaptation and mitigation will be part of our future.

A warming world, most climate scientists agree, is almost certainly responsible for the extreme weather events, hurricanes among them, that have been widely reported and experienced by many in recent years. But there is an important distinction to be made between the number and severity of storms, for example, and the extent of the economic costs exacted by them. The damage caused by hurricanes has without doubt increased dramatically, but for reasons that have as much to do with settlement patterns as carbon emissions. Florida experienced eighteen major hurricanes between 1900 and 1959 and just eleven from 1960 to 2018. But the coastal population of Florida today is sixty-seven times what it was in 1900. A hurricane ripping through only Dade and Broward Counties today would affect more people than lived along the entire coast from Texas to Virginia in 1940. The damage caused in Miami by the Great Hurricane of 1926 was $1.6 billion, in adjusted dollars. If a storm of that magnitude hammered the city today, the cost would be more like $265 billion.

In 2023, smoke from a record number of forest fires in Canada enveloped the Eastern Seaboard of the United States, rendering the air hazardous and invoking truly apocalyptic images in cities from New York to Washington, D.C. Across Canada, from Nova Scotia to British Columbia, some ten thousand square miles had burned by early June, normally just the beginning of a fourteen-week fire season that runs through mid-September. Altogether, fires in the terrible summer of 2023 would burn an unprecedented sixty-five thousand square miles. Here surely was evidence of climate change on a scale that would oblige governments to act and people to change their ways. Perhaps so, and all for the good, even if 2023 turns out to have been just a particularly bad fire season.

As tracked by the Canadian National Fire Database, the extent of forested land lost to fire has ranged from 23,000 square miles in 1981 and well over 29,000 square miles in 1989 and 1995 to 2,000 square miles in 2001, 15,000 square miles in 2013, with a low of just 1,200 square miles in 2020. Such fluctuations over four decades suggest at least the possibility that factors in addition to global warming are in play. Significantly, Canadian government data indicate that between 1980 and 2021, even as carbon emissions and global temperatures have increased, both the number of forest fires and the extent of area burned have, in fact, declined. The anomalous scale of the 2023 fires—which burned six times the long-term average of 10,500 square miles a year—was horrific but not necessarily indicative of a new norm.

Land consumed by wildfires in the western states and Alaska has increased from an average of three million acres in the 1980s to seven million in the 2010s. But in the 1930s, the average was 39 million acres. According to research published in *Science*, global fire has declined more than 25 percent since 2003, with 2020 having been one of the least active years in the fire record. That said, the number of homes built in high-risk zones in the U.S. alone has increased from half a million in 1940 to seven million in 2010. The coastal population of California has increased by six million since 2000. Eighty percent of wildfires in the United States are started by people. The grassland fires in 2021 that ravaged communities outside Boulder, Colorado, destroyed one thousand

homes that were not there a generation ago. Rising temperatures may have fueled the Maui fires in 2023 that destroyed
Lahaina, killing 115 Hawaiians, but ultimate responsibility for
the tragedy lies with the private utility that failed to maintain power lines, state and local authorities that abandoned
old dams and water storage infrastructure, and an emergency
officer who elected not to sound warning sirens. As with hurricanes and coastal flooding, the best way to manage wildfires
and reduce loss may be to focus on other human behavior as
much as our carbon emissions.

If you live in a rich country, going vegetarian will reduce
your carbon footprint by about 2 percent. Given the volume
of methane released to the atmosphere by cattle, not to mention the acreage of primary forests transformed each year
into pasture, such a gesture is surely a wise personal choice.
Unfortunately, it may be more symbolic than effective in
combatting climate change. If every American became vegetarian, U.S. emissions would decline by 5 percent; if by 2050
meat was completely expunged from the human diet, global
emissions would drop by 10 percent. The world currently has
1.5 billion vegetarians, but not all avoid meat by choice or religious conviction. Many simply can't afford it; as they move
out of poverty, consumption of animal protein will almost
certainly increase. Going vegan may be good for the health,
but it's not likely to change the world, unless the entire global
population agrees to abandon aspirations for a diet long
deemed to be a sign of economic prosperity. This may not be
right, or even logical, but humans are not driven by reason
alone.

By the same token, if all those getting on a commercial
flight this year stayed on the ground, and the same happened until the end of the century, the rise in temperatures

would be reduced by just 0.03 degrees Celsius, delaying the impact of climate change by less than a year. Avoiding non-essential travel is a personal choice, but it won't stop airlines from expanding to serve the 80 percent of the global population that has never flown, the many millions keen to experience the mobility that those in the industrialized north have enjoyed for two generations. India, the world's fastest-growing aviation market, has thirty-nine airlines. In 2023, just two of these, Air India and the budget carrier Indigo, placed orders with Boeing and Airbus for nearly a thousand passenger jets. Indigo's purchase of five hundred Airbus A320 planes was the biggest deal in the history of commercial flight. Altogether, the world's airlines are expected to acquire 42,600 new jetliners by 2042. Clearly, instead of urging people not to fly, we should focus on the carbon efficiency of airplanes, with the ultimate goal of battery-powered flight.

In considering all of these narratives, from polar bears to jet planes, I am not for a moment suggesting that rising sea levels, melting ice, extreme weather, and wildfires are not serious concerns, or that they have no causal connection to anthropocentric climate change. Quite to the contrary. The fires that flared across Canada in the summer of 2023 released to the atmosphere an estimated 1.5 billion tons of carbon dioxide, nearly three times the annual emissions of the country. Nor am I trivializing or dismissing the importance of personal agency when it comes to diet, air travel, and other efforts to reduce one's carbon footprint. Ethical decisions taken by the individual once compounded by similar choices made by others are the very drivers of social change.

But to be effective, especially in allocating capital, both financial and political, it is essential to distinguish what can be achieved from what may lie beyond our control. In the early years of the climate movement, talk of mitigation and adaptation was seen as defeatist, a form of climate denial that distracted from the essential goal of cutting emissions and eliminating fossil fuels. Writing in 1992, Al Gore dismissed adaptation as a "kind of laziness, an arrogant faith in our ability to react in time to save our skins." Reaching net zero remains a singular obsession; hence our faith in electric cars, meatless diets, and self-imposed travel restrictions, none of which, as I've suggested, is likely to realize its promise, given the many factors at play. If we are prepared to see the world as it is, as opposed to how we'd like it to be, then adaptation and mitigation stand out as essential strategies, just as economic development paradoxically offers the most viable pathway to climate resilience.

This brings us to the real elephant in the room—the cost of transformation. If we are truly faced with extinction, it appears almost unseemly to mention money. What can it matter if the fate of the planet is at stake? But if we consider global warming and climate change as a problem to be solved, with the goal of making the world a better place for all people, and indeed all creation, then cost-benefit analysis becomes essential.

The energy infrastructure that has been the foundation for two centuries of massive economic growth can be changed, but at a very high price. According to Goldman Sachs, establishing a support network for electric cars will alone cost $6 trillion, 8 percent of today's global gross domestic product. *Nature* reports that achieving a 95 percent reduction in U.S. carbon emissions by 2050 will cost 11.9 percent of U.S. GDP, more than total 2019 expenditures on Social Security, Medicare, and Medicaid.

The scale of such numbers is difficult to comprehend. In 2020 alone, largely in response to the pandemic, U.S. debt rose by $4.5 trillion. The Biden administration now proposes to spend another $2 trillion over four years on climate. The cost of Biden's proposal to eliminate emissions by 2050 breaks down to $11,000 per citizen per year. Polls suggest that even as two-thirds of Americans consider climate a major problem and believe that governments are underperforming, less than half are prepared to spend as little as $24 per capita to address it. A survey conducted in 2018 by the Associated Press and the University of Chicago found that only 16 percent of Americans were willing to pay as much as $100 a month to confront the crisis; 43 percent were not prepared to pay anything at all.

New Zealand is one of the few countries that has tried to determine what it will actually cost to achieve carbon neutrality by 2050. Cutting emissions by just half, plucking the low-hanging fruit, has an estimated price tag of $19 billion a year through 2050. Getting to net zero by 2050 would be much more difficult, with anticipated costs of $61 billion a year, more than the country spends on social security, welfare, health, education, police, courts, defense, the environment, and every other part of government combined. Given the expected temperature increase by 2100, this decision to go net zero by 2050 would postpone the warming we might expect to see on January 1, 2100, by about three weeks. In other words, a unilateral decision to eliminate all emissions would have New Zealand spending well over $3 trillion to achieve by 2100 a result that will be difficult to measure or detect.

Canadian climate activists have heralded a recent plan put forward by the Royal Bank of Canada that budgets $2 trillion to bring the nation to net zero, a per capita expenditure of more than \$56,000 that would satisfy a moral imperative at the risk of having no meaningful global effect if other nations fail to enact similar policies or lack the economic capacity to do so.

This suggests another challenge: compliance. A global survey of net-zero pledges by corporations found that half had no plans whatsoever for getting there. Exxon, long a bastion of climate denial, has formally committed to reach net zero by 2050. But its pledge covers only its operations, not the emissions of the fossil fuels that it sells, which account for 85 percent of its carbon footprint, some 762 million tons of greenhouse gases each year, as much as produced by the entire nation of Germany.

Walmart, Shell, Amazon, BP, and Toyota have all declared net zero as a goal. But, like Exxon, none address the full carbon footprint of their businesses. JBS, the world's largest meat-processing company, slaughters nine million animals a day, and over the last five years, its carbon emissions have increased 50 percent. And yet it, too, has pledged to reach net zero, by 2040. Its commitment, notes the *New York Times*, is as meaningful as that of a smoker who promises to quit in twenty years. In truth, many of these companies have simply punted the problem into the future. The era of climate denial, as Michael Shellenberger suggests, has given way to a time of climate promises that corporations have no intention or even ability to fulfill.

When it comes to the nation-states, rhetoric again trumps reality. On paper, net-zero pledges address 83 percent of all carbon emissions, accounting for 91 percent of global GDP. But not a single country is on track to realize its commitment. Of the 187 nations that promised emission reductions at Paris, only seventeen have passed laws to do so. These include Japan and Canada, but also Tonga, Samoa, and North Macedonia. Every major industrial nation has failed to live up to its pledge at Paris. Of the two hundred nations at Glasgow that affirmed their commitment to limit global warning to 1.5 degrees Celsius, virtually none have policies in place to meet that goal. The IPCC warns that to reach this threshold, carbon emissions will have to be reduced by half by 2030. And yet, as UN Secretary-General Guterres has acknowledged, global emissions by the end of the decade are, in fact, expected to increase by 14 percent. In 2022, seven years after the Paris Agreement, global fossil fuel emissions reached 36.6 billion tons, a record high.

Not only are nation-states failing to honor their pledges, they are also underreporting their emissions. A 2022 report from the International Energy Agency suggests that methane emissions alone are 70 percent higher than governments acknowledge. In 2016, Malaysia released 422 million tons of greenhouse gases and yet claimed just 81 million. Forty-five countries have not submitted any figures since 2009. Algeria, a major oil and gas producer, last reported in 2000. The carbon tally has never included the oil fields of Russia and the Middle East or the nation of Libya. According to the UN, unreported global emissions add up to some 13.3 billion tons, equivalent to China's total output.

Although countries may make pledges, all that matters is implementation. But implementation, given the costs, is a formidable political challenge even with a level playing field. Certainly the twenty nations that generate 80 percent of carbon emissions need to be held accountable. Someone living in Wyoming has a carbon footprint a thousand times that of an Ethiopian. Still, to ask Americans, Canadians, Germans, or the Dutch to unilaterally move toward carbon neutrality simply because it is the right thing to do is politically a nonstarter.

And even were such nations to take the high road, setting a moral example for the rest of the world, their sacrifices would yield only modest returns. If the U.S., currently the source of 13 percent of global emissions, achieved net zero, the consequence would be a global temperature reduction of but 0.2 degrees Celsius. And even this modest success would be negated by a decade of emission increases elsewhere.

No action by the United States, Canada, or the European Union is going to stop developing nations from using fossil fuels. Nigeria, for example, has a rapidly growing population of 200 million with a per capita income one-twelfth that of the U.S. Expecting a country that depends on oil and gas for 70 percent of its budget, and 40 percent of GDP, to forgo increases in emissions to satisfy a global carbon-free agenda crafted by the wealthy of the world, former colonial powers all, is less than realistic.

The unilateral pursuit of a carbon-free future by a select number of Western nations acting in isolation can, in fact, have profound geopolitical consequences, as Russia's barbaric invasion of Ukraine has shown. To the extent that it reduced oil and gas production in North America and Europe, the push for net zero delivered a financial windfall to Vladimir Putin, allowing Russia to accumulate capital reserves to both finance his war and insulate his regime, to the extent possible, from international sanctions. As European nations embraced net zero, shuttering coal-fired power plants, their dependence on Russian natural gas only increased, just as Putin had anticipated.

Putin clearly views the climate crisis not as a planetary emergency but rather as a geopolitical opportunity for an autocratic regime that depends on oil and gas for 40 percent of its revenues and 60 percent of its exports. Europe produces 3.6 million barrels of oil a day but consumes 15 million. Each year, it produces 230 billion cubic meters of natural gas but uses 560 billion cubic meters, 425 million tons of coal but consumes some 950 million tons.

Russia, by contrast, before the invasion, produced 11 million barrels of oil a day but consumed just 3.4 million barrels, 700 billion cubic meters of natural gas a year but used 400 billion, 800 million tons of coal while consuming just 300 million tons. Russia provided Europe with 27 percent of its oil, and since 2016, its share of the natural gas market had increased from 30 to 45 percent, nearly half of Europe's total consumption. Germany was even more exposed, relying on Russia for 55 percent of its natural gas.

Increasing Europe's energy dependency has long been at the core of Putin's geopolitical strategy, his strongest point of leverage as the autocratic leader of a paper tiger—Upper Volta with nuclear weapons, as Daniel Patrick Moynihan once described the Soviet Union—today a nation with an economy smaller than that of Texas.

While the European Union earnestly pursued a carbon-free future, Putin doubled down on fossil fuels, all with the goal of dominating Europe's energy supply. As Germany shut down nuclear power plants, closed gas fields, and curbed or shuttered fracking and coal operations, Russia expanded in all energy sectors, prioritizing nuclear for domestic consumption, allowing for larger natural gas exports to Europe, and securing with every increase in market share ever greater dependence on the part of NATO members. "While we banned plastic straws," quips Michael Shellenberger, "Russia drilled and doubled nuclear energy production."

Russia did not simply watch as the climate movement in Europe and North America rejected both the nuclear option and fracking; it actively supported these campaigns, working behind the scenes against shale gas, in particular. Anders Fogh Rasmussen notes that during his tenure as secretary-general of NATO (2009 to 2014), the Russians "engaged actively with so-called non-governmental organisations—environmental organisations working against shale gas—to maintain Europe's dependence on imported Russian gas."

The Centre for European Studies, as reported by Matt Ridley, estimates that the Russian government invested some $95 million to support and empower NGOs campaigning against coalbed methane projects. Russia's goal over more than a decade was to impede U.S. natural gas production lest its soaring supply, made possible by fracking, affect global energy markets, erode the profitability of Russian operations, and reduce European dependence on Russian sources.

Leveraging power through energy lies at the heart of Putin's diplomatic agenda, be it in the halls of a UN climate conference or in the blood-soaked streets of Ukraine's broken cities. Western sanctions aside, in the first months of the war, European nations continued to purchase Russian energy, transferring roughly $1 billion a day in payments for oil and natural gas, funding the very invasion their political leaders diplomatically denounced. Sanctions intended to drive down the value of the ruble, conceived to bring the war home to the Russian people, were countered by Putin's insistence that energy purchases be denominated in rubles; every barrel of oil or volume of gas bought by the West not only paid for the war but also propped up the Russian currency.

According to the Center for Research on Energy and Clean Air, Russian revenues from fossil fuel exports to the European Union soared to $46.3 billion during the first two months of the Ukraine invasion. This was more than double the value of Russian energy imported by the EU during the same two-month period a year earlier. The instability created by Putin's war drove up oil prices, allowing Russia to make twice as much money from the same amount of oil.

While Putin has been weaponizing oil and natural gas, the focus of U.S. energy policy has been on carbon reduction, embraced to a myopic extent. With Russian forces poised to assault a free and independent nation, John Kerry, presidential climate envoy under Biden, secretary of state during the Obama administration, expressed his singular concern that a Russian invasion "could have a profound negative impact on the climate, obviously. You have a war, and obviously you're going to have massive emissions consequences to the war. But equally importantly, you're going to lose people's focus." Given the agonies of the Ukrainian people, it is hard to recall a more wooden statement from a senior American diplomat.

Rather than chastising the world for losing its focus, Kerry would do well to acknowledge, as he surely knows, that not all nations play by the same rules and that the climate crisis is not the only challenge that confronts an ever-changing and always perilous world. Lenin, a man much admired by Putin, his namesake, wrote that there are decades when nothing happens and weeks when decades happen. Ukraine surely is such an inflection point. As one observer has bitterly remarked, the Russian assault—deliberate, cynical, bloody, and brutal—may finally oblige "the free world to grow up and stop treating energy policy like a middle school project."

"Geopolitical realism and energy realism go hand in hand," notes Derek Burney, Canada's former ambassador in Washington. The goal of reaching net-zero emissions by the end of this decade or even the next, he adds, is simply not going to happen. U.S. emissions peaked in 2007 and have since declined, largely because of the rise of wind power and the success of fracking and the replacement of coal with natural gas, which emits half as much carbon dioxide, as an energy source. A shift from one fossil fuel to a more efficient one hardly implies the end of the carbon age. According to the U.S. Energy Information Administration, oil and gas will remain the country's largest source of energy in 2050 and well beyond.

China's emissions since 2000 have tripled. India has pledged a "phase down" of coal as a proportion of its energy profile, but in absolute terms coal production is expected to soar as the economy expands. The government production target for 2024 alone is one billion tons, up from 700 million the previous year. Coal generates 80 percent of India's electricity, a figure that has not changed in a decade, and 60 percent of China's. In 2040, China is expected to still be reliant on carbon for 76 percent of its energy needs. China's very capacity to endure as a nation-state is based on a social contract that has its citizens forgoing political freedom in exchange for prosperity and domestic stability; under the current regime, economy—and hence energy—will always trump the environment. In 2022 alone, the Chinese government issued permits for 168 new coal-fired power plants.

Despite being the greatest emitter of greenhouse gases with the second largest economy in the world, China continues to self-identify as a developing nation, even as it demands that the "rich" nations transfer hundreds of millions each year to help "poor" nations combat climate change. UN secretary-general António Guterres has repeatedly called upon the G20, source of 80 percent of carbon emissions, to provide the developing world with $100 billion a year. If such multilateral schemes become operational, rivers of cash will flow as often as not into the coffers of kleptocracies. What will become of cash transfers intended to assist Yemen, Democratic Republic of the Congo, Syria, Myanmar, Somalia, or Haiti to move to a carbon-free future?

Failed states, however corrupt or dystopic their regimes, remain the homelands of millions of good and decent people, living in conditions that leave little doubt that, heretical as it may be to say, climate is not our only global problem. Every year, four million people die of malnutrition, three million from AIDS, two million from a lack of potable water. Malaria infects over a billion, killing a million each year. The UN World Food Programme estimates that every year 690 million people go hungry; 45 million are threatened by famine. There are 82 million refugees and 50 million internally displaced by poverty or conflict.

Many see the climate crisis as a supreme moment that can bring us together, giving us, as Al Gore notes, "the moral capacity to take on related challenges." Others suggest that if we squander resources chasing the holy grail of climate, these challenges will not be met, and the political fallout will, if anything, further tear us apart. If fully implemented, the Paris Agreement would commit the world to spending between $1 trillion and $2 trillion a year, all with the goal of achieving by 2100 a temperature change best described as modest. The cost of lifting every man, woman, and child out of extreme poverty is said to be $100 billion. To put this in perspective, just one month's worth of the resources dedicated to climate by the terms of the Paris Agreement would be sufficient to eliminate extreme poverty in the world.

In the end, it comes down to two closely related questions. Do we consider climate change an imminent threat to civilization, with the fate of life on Earth hanging in the balance? Or, alternatively, do we see it as a serious and daunting challenge that must and will be addressed, one of many that will confront us over the coming century?

If the answer to the first question is yes, then we really are in trouble. History does not inspire confidence that the global community can act as one, if this, indeed, is what the crisis demands, as activists maintain. Given the record of inaction to date, we can only hope that the most dire forecasts will prove to be unfounded and that through innovation, mitigation, and adaptation, humans will find a path forward, even as the world changes around us, as it has always done.

In the meantime, a climate movement that invokes the apocalyptic even while setting targets that no nation or corporation has the ability or intention to meet may do more harm than good, leaving people numb with helplessness and existential despair, dissipating the very political will necessary to actually achieve the transformation that the crisis demands.

There is a middle way, one that calls for sensible and open dialogue, with the goal not just of reducing carbon emissions but of improving the well-being of all people and the natural environments in which they live. Every day around the world some 3,700 people die in car accidents, all told 1.35 million each year, a horrific loss. Reducing the speed limit to 10 miles per hour would solve the problem, but it will never happen, as the economic and personal costs would be too high. So we aim for a balance, a speed limit we can live with, literally, but not so low as to paralyze a society dependent on mobility. Climate activists who demand an immediate end to carbon emissions are as advocates of a 10-mile-per-hour speed limit, which is why their rhetoric fails to register, leaving their goals unrealized. Polemics and fear will never move people to action. Hope and the promise of a better life in a better world will.

We cannot bury the economy and expect to have the capacity to address the problem or exploit the opportunity. The way to address climate change is to unleash the free market to increase prosperity and innovation, while resisting policies that will have the opposite effect. Rather than exhaust money, resources, and political capital on quixotic attempts to meet arbitrary if not impossible goals—for example, the elimination of all emissions by a fixed date—let's invest in solutions: smart market-based carbon taxes and R & D investments in energy storage, nuclear fusion, carbon capture, geoengineering, and algae that convert carbon dioxide to produce oil that when burned will be, by definition, a net-zero emitter of carbon. What we need are tools that will allow us to remove carbon dioxide from the atmosphere, not regulations and restrictions that will legislate behavior, restrain growth, and hamper competition just when we need the best minds of the world to be more inventive, vibrant, entrepreneurial, and inspired than at any other time in the long history of our species.

The Stone Age did not end because we ran out of stones. Kerosene displaced whale oil, and just in time. Fears that London and New York would be rendered uninhabitable by horse dung faded with the automobile. The poisonous smog over the city of Los Angeles was eliminated not by a ban on traffic but through the invention of the catalytic converter. A population explosion in India did not result in famine; the nation today produces four times as much grain as it did in 1967. When the price of green energy drops below that of fossil fuels, the age of carbon will end.

We can hasten the process by eliminating the hidden subsidies for fossil fuels, which, according to a recent report from the IMF, have surged to $7 trillion, 7.2 percent of global GDP. Governments worldwide spend more money propping up oil, coal, and natural gas than they budget for education (4.3 percent of global GDP) and close to two-thirds of what they devote to health care (10.9 percent).

We can demand oversight and efficiency. Every year, through negligence and shoddy extractive practices, fossil fuel operations around the world release to the atmosphere as much natural gas as Europe burns for power. Such leakage is both shameful and readily staunched.

In 2018, Chad Frischmann of Project Drawdown gave a compelling TED Talk in which he referenced the one hundred top solutions to the climate crisis, as determined by his organization after months of study. The list was an exhilarating cascade of the unexpected, each proposal worthy of implementation even in the absence of a climate threat. Replacing hydrofluorocarbons, for example, with natural refrigerants, readily available today, would alone eliminate gigatons of greenhouse gases.

In a hungry world, fully a third of all food is not eaten. In poorer nations, the waste occurs in the supply chain, rarely in the home. Among the wealthy, the wastage is at the table. In the U.S. alone, 40 percent of all food, 108 billion pounds, the equivalent of 130 billion meals, with a value of $408 billion, is thrown away each year. Much of it ends up in landfills, where it emits methane gas as it decomposes. Food waste is responsible for 8 percent of greenhouse gases.

Critically, as Frischmann makes clear, the solutions for humanity's chronic needs serve equally to reduce the threat of global warming. If we address the problems of hunger and food security, including storage, infrastructure, and wastage, carbon emissions will dramatically decline. If women are provided with safe and effective contraceptives, allowing them to control their lives and free their potential, they will have fewer children, reducing the carbon footprint of their families. Asked to identify the single most powerful tool in reversing the long-term impact of global warming, Frischmann, without hesitation, named family planning and the education of women.

Those who insist that only by reaching net zero will we be able to turn to other problems fail to grasp that it is only by addressing such problems that we have a realistic chance of achieving carbon neutrality. Those living in extreme poverty today can hardly be expected to care about an abstract threat that awaits in the future. To make the world more prosperous and secure, we must invest in education, technology, and health care. Free trade, including support for communities adversely affected by it; childhood nutrition; the eradication of malaria, tuberculosis, and polio; and universal access to immunization, not to mention family planning and free access to contraceptives—all such efforts are today underfunded in a world where fully one-quarter of international aid goes to climate projects.

If the goal is not just to reduce emissions but to remove carbon from the atmosphere, our best course of action is to conserve and enhance the natural systems—forests and grasslands, kelp beds, peat bogs and heaths—that draw carbon dioxide from the air, sequestering carbon through the miracle of photosynthesis. Climate activists would do well to avoid the next UN Climate Change Conference and focus instead on protecting the environments where they live.

Wetlands annually capture 6.7 million tons of greenhouse gases; two million acres disappear each year. Mangroves, sea grasses, and salt marshes covering less than 1 percent of the Earth's land surface account for 50 percent of all carbon sequestered in marine sediments. We have lost 50 percent of mangroves since 1980. The boreal forests that cover much of northern Canada, Alaska, Russia, and Scandinavia sequester carbon at twice the rate of tropical forests; collectively, they comprise the greatest carbon sink on the planet. And yet, from Siberia to Saskatchewan, they are being logged on an industrial scale for pulp, in Canada largely for the production of two-ply toilet paper.

A carbon-free energy grid won't realize its promise if the clean power is used to maintain or extend patterns of consumption that lay waste to the natural world. The city of Vancouver, where I live, has with great fanfare vowed to reach net zero by 2030, even as the province of British Columbia conspires with the logging industry to produce annually 65 million cubic meters of timber, destroying each year half a million acres of forested land. Meanwhile, across central Europe, ancient forests are being ground into sawdust to form pellets marketed as wood waste and sold as a source of green energy, allowing prosperous countries in western

Europe to fulfill their commitments to renewable power. Wood, which can be as dirty as coal when burned, is Europe's largest "renewable" energy source, well ahead of wind and solar.

By some estimates, nature-based solutions have the capacity to absorb as much carbon as is generated each year through the burning of fossil fuels. Swiss researchers have calculated that more than 3.7 million square miles of land, an area the size of the United States, could be reforested without disrupting either urban growth or agricultural production. A trillion trees planted at a cost of $300 billion would absorb, according to one estimate, two-thirds of the greenhouse gases that humans have added to the atmosphere. A quixotic goal perhaps, but not unachievable. Australia has pledged to plant a billion trees by 2030; Pakistan, ten billion within a generation. Since the 1970s, China has planted fifty billion trees. And yet, in the confusion and contradictions of global climate policy, a mere 2.5 percent of funding spent on mitigating climate change goes to such proven and potent nature-based solutions.

On my last day in Copenhagen in 2009, Carter Roberts, president and CEO of the World Wildlife Fund (U.S.), summed up the situation. There were, he suggested, only four possible outcomes. If the scientists were wrong and we did nothing, little would change. If they were wrong and we nevertheless acted to mitigate the risks, the worst that could happen would be a transformation that would result in a cleaner environment, a more technologically integrated world, and a healthier planet.

If the scientists were right and we did nothing, the potential consequences would be at best bad and at worst catastrophic. If the scientific consensus held and we aggressively marshalled our financial resources and technological capacity to confront the climate crisis, we would be able to head off potential disaster and make for a better world. It was difficult to conjure a losing scenario, save that of inaction.

But to act in a manner that is meaningful, effective, and truly transformative, we need a language not of desperation and doom but of confidence and determination. On a mission to save the planet, pessimism is an indulgence, orthodoxy the enemy of invention, despair an insult to the imagination. The global energy grid will be transformed, if not in our lifetime then certainly in that of our grandchildren. The impetus and motivation will be hope, not fear; the agent of change, our human ingenuity—the adaptive capacity to innovate and invent that has always allowed our species to thrive.

12

A MESSAGE
TO A DAUGHTER

LET ME TELL YOU A STORY that begins on a ridge in Borneo, close to dusk with thunder over the valley and the forest alive with the electrifying roar of black cicadas. I was sitting by a fire with an old friend, Asik Nyelit, headman of the Ubong River Penan, one of the last nomadic peoples of Southeast Asia.

The rains, which had pounded the forest all afternoon, had stopped, and the light of a partial moon filtered through the branches of the canopy. Earlier in the day, Asik had killed a barking deer. Its head roasted in the coals.

At one point, Asik looked up from the fire, took notice of the moon, and quietly asked me if it was true that people had actually journeyed there, only to return with baskets full of dirt. If that was all they had found, why had they bothered to go?

Asik's question provoked the timeless answer. The true purpose of the space journeys, or at least their most profound and lasting consequence, lay not in wealth secured but a vision realized, a shift in perspective that would change our lives forever.

The seminal moment came on Christmas Eve, 1968, when Apollo 8 emerged from the dark side of the moon to see rising over its surface not a sunrise but the Earth itself ascendant, a small and fragile planet, floating in the velvet void of space. This image more than any amount of scientific data showed us that our planet is a finite place, a single interactive sphere of life, a living organism composed of air, water, wind, and soil. This revelation, only made possible by the brilliance of science, sparked a paradigm shift that people will be speaking about for the rest of history.

Almost immediately, we began to think in new ways. Just imagine. Fifty years ago, simply getting people to stop throwing garbage out of a car window was a great environmental victory. No one spoke of the biosphere or biodiversity; now these terms are part of the vocabulary of schoolchildren.

Like a great wave of hope, this energy of illumination spread everywhere. So many positive things have happened in the intervening years. In little more than a generation, women have gone from the kitchen to the boardroom, gay men and women from the closet to the altar, African Americans from the back door and the woodshed to the White House. What's not to love about a country and a world capable of such scientific genius, such cultural capacity for change and renewal?

But let me share one other amazing revelation of science. It's the moon shot of your generation. It, too, will be remembered in a thousand years. Nothing in our lifetimes has done more to liberate humanity from the parochial tyrannies that have haunted us since the birth of memory.

This, too, came about at the end of a long voyage of discovery, a journey into the very fiber of our beings. Over the last decade, studies of the human genome have left no doubt that the genetic endowment of humanity is a single continuum.

Race is an utter fiction. The brilliance of scientific research, the revelations of modern genetics, have affirmed in an astonishing way the essential connectedness of humanity.

We are all brothers and sisters, literally one family, all descendants of common ancestors, all ultimately children of Africa. Skin color—exploited for generations as the cruelest of human conceits—is nothing more than basic adaptation; people in tropical climes needing sunscreen, or melanin, and those living through long northern winters having to maximize sun exposure to absorb vitamin D, essential for health and well-being. Black and white in the end comes down to sunscreen and vitamin D, nothing more.

Cut from the same genetic cloth, we all share, by definition, the same intellectual capacity and potential. Words such as *primitive* and *civilized* suggest a hierarchy of culture that has never existed, save in the minds of those who benefited from such colonial and racial conceptions. Every culture is a unique expression of our shared human genius. Each has something to say that the world needs to hear.

What this means for you is very simple. There are tens of thousands of teachers out there in every corner of the world that you did not even know you had.

You can sail with Polynesian wayfinders, navigators who can sense the presence of distant atolls beyond the visible horizon simply by watching the reverberation of waves across the hull of their vessels.

You can follow the Tendai monks in Japan, who as part of their initiation run seventeen hours at a stretch every day for seven years, wearing out five pairs of sandals a day.

You can join a caravan of blue-robed Tuareg in the searing sands of the Sahara or hunt narwhal with the Inuit in the light of the midnight sun. You can sit by the side of a bodhi-sattva in a Tibetan cave or study medicine at the foot of an Amazonian shaman.

Or you can pursue completely different avenues of adventure and discovery in science, the arts, social justice, engineering, medicine, the military, or the clergy. No generation has had so many options or shown such promise.

All these grand sentiments aside, you may be wondering how any of this will help you get from where you are to where you want to be. You know you have options. What you don't know is what you want, which path to follow, what career to pursue. You excelled in university only to graduate after four years with little sense of what your liberal arts degree has prepared you to do. I know the feeling. When I left college, your grandmother asked about my plans. I confessed that I had none. It was the first and only time that I ever heard my mother scream, albeit over a phone line, reminding me, as if I didn't already know, that I was twenty-three years old.

Sincere and loving as she was, your grandmother's anguish in that moment had little to do with me. When elders have plans for your life, they are generally envisioning not you but themselves, or at least, in their disappointments, the person they had once dreamed of being. Friends, too, can be a blessing but also a barrier to growth. Friendship is all about reciprocity; friends support the person you are, which gives them comfort, but not necessarily the new and unpredictable woman emerging with every shift and surge in your fortunes. Change is unsettling, especially for those deeply invested in the status quo, meaning in Latin the "existing state of affairs."

But let me tell you about an inspirational character who most assuredly achieved a certain greatness, realizing his dreams while defying convention every step of the way. Like you, Steve graduated from college with a liberal arts degree and no idea what to do next. So he went to India, where he stayed for four years, living in a cave. He knew it was time to come home when the local people started bringing him money and food. So he came back to the States and meditated for sixty-five days, trying to figure out what to do. Suddenly he had a flash: vegetable protein!

Now the person telling this story, having shared Steve's epiphany, turned to me in a conspiratorial tone and whispered, "You know how hard that is." I had no idea what he was talking about. But Steve had figured out that the problem with soy milk was not the product but the container, which relegated it to the weird food section of the grocery store. So he changed the name, *soy* and *milk* becoming *Silk*, packaged it in milk cartons, and had it placed beside the milk in the dairy section. Five years later, Steve sold his company for $295 million.

What Steve discovered is a universal lesson. Life is neither linear nor predictable. A career is not something you put on like a coat. It is something that grows organically around you, step by step, choice by choice, and experience by experience. Everything adds up. No work is beneath you. Nothing is a waste of time unless you make it so. An elderly cab driver in New York may well have as much to teach you as a wandering saint in India, a madman in the Sahara, and most certainly a university professor.

If you place yourself in the way of opportunities, in situations where there is no choice but to move forward, no option but success, you create a momentum that in the end propels you to new levels of experience and engagement that would have seemed beyond reach only months before.

Creativity is a consequence of action, not its motivation. Do what needs to be done and then ask whether it was possible or permissible. Nature loves courage. Jim Whittaker, the first American to summit Everest, said that if you don't live on the edge when young, you're taking up too much space.

Dream the impossible, and the world will not drag you under; it will lift you up. This is the great surprise, the message of the saints. You hurl yourself into the abyss only to discover that it's a feather bed.

You are understandably concerned about finding a job. Just be careful. The word *job* is derived from the sixteenth-century French word *gober*, meaning to devour. My father had a job all of his life. He called it the grind. As a boy, I used to think that he went into the city every day and returned a little smaller.

Fortunately, I have never had a job, at least not in this sense. Actually, I have never really had a job at all. And I don't imagine you will find a single slot into which to plug your entire existence.

But what you will do is work, no doubt as ferociously hard as I have all my life. The word *work* has a better ring to it. It comes from the Old English, meaning action and deed.

And you'll find that the work you do is just a lens through which to view and experience the world, and only for a time.

The goal is to make living itself, the act of being alive, one's vocation, knowing full well that nothing ultimately can be planned or anticipated, no blueprint found to predict the outcome of something as complex as a human life.

If one can remain open to the potential of the new, the promise of the unimagined, then magic happens and a life takes form. The best of things come from those incapable of compromise. It takes time for an individual to create a new world of possibilities, to imagine and bring into being that which has never before existed, the wonder of a full and realized life.

And you have so much time. At twenty, your life is just beginning. Your great-grandmother could expect to live until sixty-two, her husband to fifty-eight. The retirement age was set at sixty-five, only because by then most would be dead and governments would not have to pay the benefits they had promised workers to quell labor unrest in the nineteenth century. Sixty-five has nothing to do with you. Your life expectancy is closer to ninety-five. So many years to go, and so many adventures to be had.

As you make your way, please give as much thought to the person you will become as to the vocation you will pursue. Money in the end means very little. Acts of compassion and loving kindness resonate through eternity.

My father, who died before you were born, wasn't a religious man, but he believed in good and evil. So did your grandmother, but in a different way. Though she, too, had turned away from the church, some part of her retained faith that if we just tried hard enough, good would ultimately triumph over evil, just as Christ, the son of God, was destined to vanquish the Devil, the fallen archangel. Your grandfather had no such illusions. "There's good and evil in the world," he would say. "Pick your side and get on with it."

There was great wisdom in this advice. Good and evil, as history makes clear, march side by side. They always have and always will. We can never defeat darkness. We can only do what's right, without expecting to win or to lose. With no expectations, there can be no disappointment and no reason to abandon the fight. The long march of life is a pilgrim's path. The goal is not a destination, but a state of mind.

When I was young, living in the mountains of Colombia, a Kamsa man told me something I have never forgotten. "In the first years of your life," Pedro said, "you live beneath the shadow of the past, too young to know what to do. In your last years, you find that you are too old to understand the world coming at you from behind. In between, there is a small and narrow beam of light that illuminates your life."

If you can look back over a long life and see that you have owned your choices, then there is little ground for resentment. Bitterness comes to those who look back with regret on the choices imposed upon them. The greatest creative challenge is the struggle to be the architect of your own life. So be patient. Do not compromise. And give your destiny time to find you.

13

ON THE SACRED

AS A BOY I PRAYED EVERY NIGHT, hands together, elbows perched on the sill of a bedroom window open to the winter air, eyes wide to the stars sparkling through the branches of the giant elm trees that in those years still thrived in the neighborhoods of old Quebec. I conversed with a God whose presence could be felt and whose spiritual authority and omnipotence I accepted as an act of faith.

My parents, broken by the war, rarely saw the inside of a church. So, from the age of six, I dutifully set off every Sunday on my own and continued to do so without fail for five years. I still have the gold pin with the silver cross that rewarded my attendance record. Like a pilgrim at the gates of a great cathedral, I didn't attend service to worship the building; I went there to be in the presence of God. For a long time, he was always to be found. But, as the years went by and I learned more and more about the world, there came a day when he simply failed to show. I never again entered a church as a Christian believer.

When, years later, I returned to that small community as an adult, what astonished me most was how small my universe had been and how intimately I had known it. Every blade of grass resonated with a story. Shadows marked the ground where trees had fallen in my absence. Innovations and new construction I took as personal insults, violations of something sacred that lay at the confluence of landscape and memory.

What I felt so powerfully in that moment was not nostalgia but rather a connection to the actual force that for all those years had propelled my spiritual yearning, a numinous energy that, thanks to my friend Shefa Siegel, I now recognize as being the essence of the sacred, the invisible presence that the French philosopher Henry Corbin described as the imaginal, a suprasensory dimension that transcends religion, a space of intuition and revelation impossible to describe yet accessible to those in every culture who perceive the world, as Corbin wrote, "through the eyes of the heart."

My longings as a child, I realized, had not been of a religious nature, at least not in a formal sense; I'd been looking for a path that embraced the mystic among the multitudes, the promise of all people in all places through all time who had found peace and comfort in their pursuit of the divine. I came to see God as but the product of our desires. Our spirit and imagination transform an edifice of stone into a sacred space. A shrine is sanctified by the legacy of all those who have come before, with their hopes, fears, promises, and prayers.

Relics, icons, chalices, and crosses—all simple objects crafted from wood, silver, and bone—take on spiritual resonance only over time, like old tools warm from decades of human touch.

Sacrifice means to make sacred, and if the idea of the sacred is as old as human awareness, as anthropology suggests, then the sacred can never be divorced from human agency. We dream the sacred into being. Ritual is the ground from which it springs. The sacred becomes manifest through the enactment of rituals that summon the spirit and give form to the divine.

In Haiti, the waterfall at Saut d'Eau is the home of Damballah Wedo, the serpent god, repository of spiritual wisdom and the source of the falling waters. When the first rains fell, a rainbow, Ayida Wedo, was reflected. Damballah fell in love with Ayida, and their love entwined them in a cosmic helix from which all creation was fertilized. Every summer, over three days in July, as many as fifteen thousand pilgrims, all devotees of the Lwa, the spirits of the Vodoun pantheon, make their way to the sacred site. One need only touch the water to feel its grace, and for some it is enough to dip into the shallow silvery pools. But most go directly to the cascades, men and women, old and young, baring their breasts and scrambling up the slippery bedrock that rises in a series of steps toward the base of the falls. Merely to submit to the waters is to open oneself to Damballah, and at any one time at the base of the waterfall in the shadow of the rainbow, there are a hundred or more pilgrims possessed by the spirit, slithering across the wet rocks.

For most of the year, the Sinakara Valley in the southern Andes of Peru is home only to solitary shepherds and their flocks. But for three days between the feast of the Ascension and Corpus Christi, as the Pleiades re-emerge in the night sky, as many as forty thousand pilgrims converge at the base of the mountain to take part in the Qoyllur Rit'i, the Star Snow Festival. Some arrive on foot, some by mule, and others in open trucks and buses. The pilgrims make their way up a trail that climbs for seven miles, a route marked by altars and cairns, the stations of the cross, where men and women pause to pray and make offerings. Each pilgrim carries a bundle of small stones, a symbolic burden of sin to be lightened one by one as the valley comes near.

It falls upon ritual specialists, the *pablitos*, to perform the most dangerous and solemn act of the Qoyllur Rit'i. Like Christ himself, they shoulder a terrible burden, carrying the crosses from their village churches up the flanks to the ice fields of the Colquepunku, where they implant them in the snow to be charged by the energy of the mountain and the earth. Then, before dawn on the morning of the third day, roped together by whips, they climb back to the ice to retrieve the crosses as, far below, thousands of pilgrims kneel in silent prayer. All eyes are on the summit, in homage to the Apus, the mountain deities.

As the sun comes up, the crosses come down and make their way on the backs of the pilgrims through the Sinakara and out through the pass, into the trucks that will take them back to the villages. The men also carry from the mountain small blocks of ice, which completes the devotional cycle: the people go to the mountain; the essence of the mountain returns to the villages to bring fertility to the fields, well-being to the families, health to the animals. Pilgrimage through sacred geography, homage to the gods, becomes a collective prayer for the cultural survival of the entire pan-Andean world.

When the first humans reached the shores of Australia, they went walking, establishing in time more than ten thousand clan territories, independent homelands all bound together by the Songlines, the tracks followed by the primordial ancestors who, in the time of the Rainbow Serpent, sang the world into being. As Aboriginal people today trace the Songlines and chant the stories of the first dawning, they enter the Dreamtime, which is neither a dream nor a measure of the passage of time. It is the very realm of the ancestors, a parallel universe where the ordinary laws of time, space, and motion do not apply, where past, future, and present merge into one.

To walk the Songlines is to become part of the ongoing creation of the world, a place that both exists and is still being formed. Thus, Aboriginal peoples are not merely attached to the earth, they are essential to its existence. Without the land, they would die. But without the people, the earth would wither. Should the rituals stop, the voices fall silent, all would be lost. Everything on earth is held together by the Songlines, just as everything is subordinate to the Dreaming, which is constant but ever-changing. Every landmark is wedded to a memory of its origins and yet always in the process of being born. Every animal and object resonates with the pulse of an ancient event, while still being dreamed into being. The land is encoded with everything that has ever been, everything that ever will be, in every dimension of reality. The world is perfect, though constantly being reimagined and renewed. To walk the land and honor the Songlines is to engage in a constant act of affirmation, an endless dance of creation.

The most profound cultural insight of the Barasana and Makuna, whose lives unfold in the forests of the Colombian Amazon, is the realization that plants and animals are but people in another dimension of reality. Mythology infuses land and life with meaning. Ritual reinforces the norms that drive social behavior, encoding expectations and behaviors essential to survival in the forest. There is no separation between nature and culture. Without the forest and the rivers, humans would perish. But without people, the natural world would have no order or meaning. All would be chaos.

Maintaining the flow of generative energy, fomenting reciprocity among all forms of life, is the duty of the shaman, who is neither priest nor physician; he is a diplomat in constant dialogue with the spirit realm, with all the responsibilities of a nuclear engineer who must, if necessary, enter the heart of the reactor and reprogram the world. The shaman moves with ease through mystical dimensions unseen by ordinary eyes but familiar to the Barasana and Makuna, who say that they see with their minds. In ritual ceremonies that embrace the entire community, the men come together to ingest yagé, a powerful potion that serves as a portal to the divine. As they don the ritual regalia, the yellow corona of pure thought, the white egret plumes of the rain, they become the ancestors, reliving their mythic journeys, alighting on all the sacred sites, transcending every form, becoming as if a single pulse of pure energy flowing through all of creation.

Each of these stories, these cultural accounts, is rooted in place, the product of a particular way of thinking, a unique vision of life itself. But they all express a common impulse: a fundamental human desire to engage not death but life as it is, the invisible forces that lie all around us, the realm of the imaginal in the here and now. Death, of course, is the great mystery, the edge beyond which life as we know it ends and wonder begins. How a culture comes to terms with the inexorable separation that death implies invariably determines its religious worldview. Stripped to the bone, most religious longings and traditions come down to a simple desire to wrestle with eternity and come out on top. The pursuit and embrace of the sacred, by contrast, has nothing to do with death; it is all about life.

The sacred is eternal, reaching far into the past, shining as a beacon to the future. It is everywhere and nowhere. What is sacred can never be diluted or compromised, co-opted or copied, commodified or made sordid through commerce and greed. Sensed if never seen, elusive and mysterious by its very nature, the sacred may lie beyond our reach, yet there is comfort just in knowing that such a radiant presence may one day be encountered. The clock is not ticking. No force exists that can rob us of its promise. The traveler today walks the same spiritual ground as the pilgrim of old.

When I was a boy, still in the thrall of my Christian faith, my father, without being unkind, gently dismissed religion as wishful thinking; every church, he quipped, ought to have a billboard outside with the cautionary words "Important, if true." Perhaps he was right. But the pursuit of the sacred, as I discovered long ago, has nothing to do with religion. It is not concerned with what lies beyond death; it makes, in fact, no claims to anything at all. The sacred embodies and radiates the glory of what exists in this moment, on this blue jewel of a planet. "Before Buddha or Jesus spoke," wrote D. H. Lawrence, "the nightingale sang, and long after the words of Jesus and Buddha are gone into oblivion the nightingale still will sing." The goal of the pilgrim is to become as if a bird "dissolved in the sky yet filling heaven and earth with song." Passing through the sky, leaving no trace, at one with the sacred.

ACKNOWLEDGMENTS

I WOULD FIRST like to thank the many inspired editors from various publications who worked with me on these essays: Amanda Betts, Mandy Kirkby, Cameron Lamb, Tim Martin, Phoebe Neidl, Gillian Tett, Dan Vergano, Gus Wenner, Kate Wilkinson, Sean Woods, and Kyle Wyatt. Friends and colleagues who read some or all of the essays and offered helpful advice include Ajaz Ahmed, Ross Beaty, Trisha Beaty, Andrew Cockburn, Lavinia Currier, Simon Davies, Karen Davis, Louise Dennys, Claire Enders, David Freeman, Ginny Freeman, James Gaines, David Ignatius, Steven King, Steven Koonin, Michael Levine, Ian Mackenzie, Corky McIntyre, Scott McIntyre, Olivia McKendrick, Gail Percy, Mark Percy, Christopher Pollon, Travis Price, Alexander Rafael, Chris Rainier, Bob Ramsay, Johan Reinhard, Shefa Siegel, Dan Taylor, Tomás Uribe, Xandra Uribe, Andrew Weil, Jann Wenner, and Ric Young.

My thanks to the excellent team at Greystone: Paula Ayer, Crissy Calhoun, Jennifer Croll, Nancy Flight, Jen Gauthier, Megan Jones, Rob Sanders, Jennifer Stewart, and Jessica Sullivan. Finally, a very special thanks to Pico Iyer who generously helped me find a title, and to Jann Wenner who has inspired me on this and so many other projects over the years. As always, my gratitude to my family, the anchor in a wayward life.

WADE DAVIS served as Explorer-in-Residence at the National Geographic Society from 2000–2013 and is currently Professor of Anthropology at the University of British Columbia. His twenty-four books, published in twenty-three languages, include the international bestsellers *The Serpent and the Rainbow*, *One River*, *The Wayfinders*, and *Into the Silence*, winner of the 2012 Samuel Johnson Prize, the top nonfiction award in the English language.